Linda Ronstadt

Linda Ronstadt

Melissa Amdur

CHELSEA HOUSE PUBLISHERS
PHILADELPHIA

CHELSEA HOUSE PUBLISHERS

Editorial Director: Richard Rennert
Executive Managing Editor: Karyn Gullen Browne
Executive Editor: Sean Dolan
Copy Chief: Robin James
Picture Editor: Adrian G. Allen
Manufacturing Director: Gerald Levine
Systems Manager: Lindsey Ottman
Production Coordinator: Marie Claire Cebrián-Ume

HISPANICS OF ACHIEVEMENT
Senior Editor: Philip Koslow

Staff for *LINDA RONSTADT*
Designer: M. Cambraia Magalhaes
Picture Researcher: Lisa Kirshner
Cover Illustrator: Daniel O'Leary

5 7 9 8 6

Library of Congress Cataloging-in-Publication Data
Amdur, Melissa.
Linda Ronstadt/Melissa Amdur.
p. cm.—(Hispanics of Achievement)
Includes bibliographical references and index.
Summary: Examines the life and musical career of the female singer whose
performances have included rock, opera, and Mexican folk music.
ISBN 0-7910-1781-8
0-7910-2025-8 (pbk.)
1. Ronstadt, Linda—Juvenile literature. 2. Singers—United States—Biography—
Juvenile literature. [1. Ronstadt, Linda. 2. Singers. 3. Mexican Americans—Biog-
raphy.] I. Title. II. Series.
92-37186
ML3930.R65A8 1993
CIP
782.42164'092—dc20
[B]
AC MN

CONTENTS

Hispanics of Achievement   7

Canciones de Mi Padre   15

Border Crossings   21

A Different Drum   31

Heart Like a Wheel   43

Linda in Disguise   55

The Pirate Queen   67

From Pop to Puccini   81

The Songs of Her Father   97

Selected Discography   106

Chronology   107

Further Reading   109

Index   110

HISPANICS OF ACHIEVEMENT

JOAN BAEZ
Mexican-American folksinger

RUBÉN BLADES
Panamanian lawyer and entertainer

JORGE LUIS BORGES
Argentine writer

PABLO CASALS
Spanish cellist and conductor

MIGUEL DE CERVANTES
Spanish writer

CESAR CHAVEZ
Mexican-American labor leader

EL CID
Spanish military leader

ROBERTO CLEMENTE
Puerto Rican baseball player

SALVADOR DALÍ
Spanish painter

PLÁCIDO DOMINGO
Spanish singer

GLORIA ESTEFAN
Cuban-American singer

JULIO IGLESIAS
Spanish singer

RAUL JULIA
Puerto Rican actor

GABRIEL GARCÍA MÁRQUEZ
Colombian writer

FRANCISCO JOSÉ DE GOYA
Spanish painter

FRIDA KAHLO
Mexican painter

JOSÉ MARTÍ
Cuban revolutionary and poet

RITA MORENO
Puerto Rican singer and actress

PABLO NERUDA
Chilean poet and diplomat

ANTONIA NOVELLO
U.S. surgeon general

OCTAVIO PAZ
Mexican poet and critic

PABLO PICASSO
Spanish artist

ANTHONY QUINN
Mexican-American actor

DIEGO RIVERA
Mexican painter

LINDA RONSTADT
Mexican-American singer

ANTONIO LÓPEZ DE SANTA ANNA
Mexican general and politician

GEORGE SANTAYANA
Spanish philosopher and poet

JUNÍPERO SERRA
Spanish missionary and explorer

LEE TREVINO
Mexican-American golfer

DIEGO VELÁZQUEZ
Spanish painter

PANCHO VILLA
Mexican revolutionary

CHELSEA HOUSE PUBLISHERS

HISPANICS OF ACHIEVEMENT

Rodolfo Cardona

The Spanish language and many other elements of Spanish culture are present in the United States today and have been since the country's earliest beginnings. Some of these elements have come directly from the Iberian Peninsula; others have come indirectly, by way of Mexico, the Caribbean basin, and the countries of Central and South America.

Spanish culture has influenced America in many subtle ways, and consequently many Americans remain relatively unaware of the extent of its impact. The vast majority of them recognize the influence of Spanish culture in America, but they often do not realize the great importance and long history of that influence. This is partly because Americans have tended to judge the Hispanic influence in the United States in statistical terms rather than to look closely at the ways in which individual Hispanics have profoundly affected American culture. For this reason, it is fitting that Americans obtain more than a passing acquaintance with the origins of these Spanish cultural elements and gain an understanding of how they have been woven into the fabric of American society.

It is well documented that Spanish seafarers were the first to explore and colonize many of the early territories of what is today called the United States of America. For this reason, students of geography discover Hispanic names all over the map of the United States. For instance, the Strait of Juan de Fuca was named after the Spanish explorer who first navigated the waters of the Pacific Northwest; the names of states such as Arizona (arid zone), Montana (mountain), Florida (thus named because it was reached on Easter Sunday, which in Spanish is called the feast of Pascua Florida), and California (named after a fictitious land in one of the first and probably the most popular among the Spanish novels of chivalry, *Amadis of Gaul*) are all derived from Spanish; and there are numerous mountains, rivers, canyons, towns, and cities with Spanish names throughout the United States.

Not only explorers but many other illustrious figures in Spanish history have helped define American culture. For example, the 13th-century king of Spain, Alfonso X, also known as the Learned, may be unknown to the majority of Americans, but his work on the codification of Spanish law has greatly influenced the evolution of American law, particularly in the jurisdictions of the Southwest. For this contribution a statue of him stands in the rotunda of the Capitol in Washington, D.C. Likewise, the name Diego Rivera may be unfamiliar to most Americans, but this Mexican painter influenced many American artists whose paintings, commissioned during the Great Depression and the New Deal era of the 1930s, adorn the walls of government buildings throughout the United States. In recent years the contributions of Puerto Ricans, Mexicans, Mexican Americans (Chicanos), and Cubans in American cities such as Boston, Chicago, Los Angeles, Miami, Minneapolis, New York, and San Antonio have been enormous.

The importance of the Spanish language in this vast cultural complex cannot be overstated. Spanish, after all, is second only to English as the most widely spoken of Western languages within the United States as well as in the entire world. The popularity of the Spanish language in America has a long history.

In addition to Spanish exploration of the New World, the great Spanish literary tradition served as a vehicle for bringing the language and culture to America. Interest in Spanish literature in America began when English immigrants brought with them translations of Spanish masterpieces of the Golden Age. As early as 1683, private libraries in Philadelphia and Boston contained copies of the first picaresque novel, *Lazarillo de Tormes*, translations of Francisco de Quevedo's *Los Sueños*, and copies of the immortal epic of reality and illusion *Don Quixote*, by the great Spanish writer Miguel de Cervantes. It would not be surprising if Cotton Mather, the arch-Puritan, read *Don Quixote* in its original Spanish, if only to enrich his vocabulary in preparation for his writing *La fe del cristiano en 24 artículos de la Institución de Cristo, enviada a los españoles para que abran sus ojos* (The Christian's Faith in 24 Articles of the Institution of Christ, Sent to the Spaniards to Open Their Eyes), published in Boston in 1699.

Over the years, Spanish authors and their works have had a vast influence on American literature—from Washington Irving, John Steinbeck, and Ernest Hemingway in the novel to Henry Wadsworth Longfellow and Archibald MacLeish in poetry. Such important American writers as James Fenimore Cooper, Edgar Allan Poe, Walt Whitman, Mark Twain, and Herman Melville all owe a sizable debt to the Spanish literary tradition. Some writers, such as Willa Cather and Maxwell Anderson, who explored Spanish themes they came into contact with in the American Southwest and Mexico, were influenced less directly but no less profoundly.

Important contributions to a knowledge of Spanish culture in the United States were also made by many lesser known individuals—teachers, publishers, historians, entrepreneurs, and others—with a love for Spanish culture. One of the most significant of these contributions was made by Abiel Smith, a Harvard College graduate of the class of 1764, when he bequeathed stock worth $20,000 to Harvard for the support of a professor of French and Spanish. By 1819 this endowment had produced enough income to appoint a professor, and the philologist and humanist George Ticknor became the first holder of the Abiel

Smith Chair, which was the very first endowed Chair at Harvard University. Other illustrious holders of the Smith Chair would include the poets Henry Wadsworth Longfellow and James Russell Lowell.

A highly respected teacher and scholar, Ticknor was also a collector of Spanish books, and as such he made a very special contribution to America's knowledge of Spanish culture. He was instrumental in amassing for Harvard libraries one of the first and most impressive collections of Spanish books in the United States. He also had a valuable personal collection of Spanish books and manuscripts, which he bequeathed to the Boston Public Library.

With the creation of the Abiel Smith Chair, Spanish language and literature courses became part of the curriculum at Harvard, which also went on to become the first American university to offer graduate studies in Romance languages. Other colleges and universities throughout the United States gradually followed Harvard's example, and today Spanish language and culture may be studied at most American institutions of higher learning.

No discussion of the Spanish influence in the United States, however brief, would be complete without a mention of the Spanish influence on art. Important American artists such as John Singer Sargent, James A. M. Whistler, Thomas Eakins, and Mary Cassatt all explored Spanish subjects and experimented with Spanish techniques. Virtually every serious American artist living today has studied the work of the Spanish masters as well as the great 20th-century Spanish painters Salvador Dalí, Joan Miró, and Pablo Picasso.

The most pervasive Spanish influence in America, however, has probably been in music. Compositions such as Leonard Bernstein's *West Side Story*, the Latinization of William Shakespeare's *Romeo and Juliet* set in New York's Puerto Rican quarter, and Aaron Copland's *Salon Mexico* are two obvious examples. In general, one can hear the influence of Latin rhythms—from tango to mambo, from guaracha to salsa—in virtually every form of American music.

This series of biographies, which Chelsea House has published under the general title HISPANICS OF ACHIEVEMENT, constitutes further recognition of—and a renewed effort to bring forth to the consciousness of America's young people—the contributions that Hispanic people have made not only in the United States but throughout the civilized world. The men and women who are featured in this series have attained a high level of accomplishment in their respective fields of endeavor and have made a permanent mark on American society.

The title of this series must be understood in its broadest possible sense: The term *Hispanics* is intended to include Spaniards, Spanish Americans, and individuals from many countries whose language and culture have either direct or indirect Spanish origins. The names of many of the people included in this series will be immediately familiar; others will be less recognizable. All, however, have attained recognition within their own countries, and often their fame has transcended their borders.

The series HISPANICS OF ACHIEVEMENT thus addresses the attainments and struggles of Hispanic people in the United States and seeks to tell the stories of individuals whose personal and professional lives in some way reflect the larger Hispanic experience. These stories are exemplary of what human beings can accomplish, often against daunting odds and by extraordinary personal sacrifice, where there is conviction and determination. Fray Junípero Serra, the 18th-century Spanish Franciscan missionary, is one such individual. Although in very poor health, he devoted the last 15 years of his life to the foundation of missions throughout California—then a mostly unsettled expanse of land—in an effort to bring a better life to Native Americans through the cultivation of crafts and animal husbandry. An example from recent times, the Mexican-American labor leader Cesar Chavez has battled bitter opposition and made untold personal sacrifices in his effort to help poor agricultural workers who have been exploited for decades on farms throughout the Southwest.

The talent with which each one of these men and women may have been endowed required dedication and hard work to develop and become fully realized. Many of them have enjoyed rewards for their efforts during their own lifetime, whereas others have died poor and unrecognized. For some it took a long time to achieve their goals, for others success came at an early age, and for still others the struggle continues. All of them, however, stand out as people whose lives have made a difference, whose achievements we need to recognize today and should continue to honor in the future.

Linda Ronstadt

CANCIONES DE MI PADRE

The lights go down in Manhattan's glittering City Center theater as a spotlight picks out an enormous sombrero, painted in bright colors on a black velvet curtain. Suddenly, the velvet curtain is whisked off to the right of the stage, helped along by a smiling dancer with ribbons in her hair. As the stage is revealed, a huge fan with intricate decorations unfolds behind a veritable army of mariachi musicians, who begin to play the lively first song. As the music fills the auditorium, another figure emerges from behind the musicians. Dressed in a beaded torera jacket and long skirt, a woman with large red roses framing her face strides to the edge of the stage. Her voice fills the theater, and the audience leaps to its feet and applauds excitedly.

Linda Ronstadt acknowledges her accolades with a slight bow and a wide smile as she sings "Por un Amor" ("For a Love"), a vigorous, almost upbeat lament of lost love. Her vocal skills are so breathtaking in person that it takes some time for the sellout crowd to calm down and really listen. From the look and sound of things, Linda Ronstadt has scaled new heights of accomplishment with her show, Canciones

Linda Ronstadt's musical career has been one of relentless artistic growth, enriched by her willingness to use a variety of musical styles—rock 'n' roll, country, standards, opera, and the folk music of her Mexican heritage.

15

de Mi Padre (Songs of My Father): A Romantic Evening in Old Mexico. Never before has she seemed so happy and self-possessed on stage, or so comfortable with her singing and in sync with her musicians.

After many years of careful thought and planning, Canciones de Mi Padre had been created first as an album, long awaited and praised highly by critics on its release. Reviewers commented that the album sounded as though it was the most deeply felt of her career and that her talent had never before seemed so formidable. The show grew out of the touring process that had always been one of the foundations of Ronstadt's work. She enjoyed both the rewards and discomforts of touring and had always been deeply committed to bringing her music to as many people as possible. Ronstadt herself conceived of Canciones de Mi Padre as a theatrical glimpse of the romance that was so much a part of Mexican entertainment during the 1920s and 1930s. Her aunt, a performer of that era who was known as Luisa Espinel, captured the essence of that vanished time when she wrote in the

Ronstadt's interest in mariachi and ranchera music was inspired in large part by the career of her aunt, Luisa Espinel, who had been a popular performer of Mexican music in the 1920s and 1930s.

1940s that the sweetness of the music had "the fragrance of wildflowers dried in herbs." In fact, Ronstadt's own stage show was created along the outlines of the performances Luisa Espinel had given as a young singer and dancer many decades before. The presentation of the songs, displays of formal dancing styles, costume changes, and other theatrical flourishes all had their roots in the great Mexican musical tradition.

Another backdrop slides away to reveal a beautiful, pastel desertscape. The lighting is dreamy and mellow, casting soft shadows across the 13 members of the foremost mariachi band in the world, Mariachi Vargas de Tecalitlán. They raise their oversize stringed instruments and horns to begin another song as Ronstadt steps out among them, appearing in a new guise. Wearing a white blouse embroidered with multi-colored flowers and a full skirt, she begins to sing "Hay Unos Ojos," a slow, sweet love ballad. Long black braids trail down to her waist as she sits down beside Daniel Valdez, a mariachi playing an oversize *guitarra*, under a huge cartoon moon. As the song languorously draws to a close, Valdez leans over Ronstadt, obscuring her face with the wide brim of his sombrero as he bestows a kiss. Suddenly, the stage is a blur of white as members of the Ballet Folklórico de la Fonda rush gracefully on to perform an elaborate courting dance to "La Bamba," the tune rock singer Ritchie Valens made a hit during the 1950s. An old and traditional melody, "La Bamba" was customarily played for young couples who were just getting to know each other. The dancers whirl in perfect unison across the stage, relaxed yet still full of the vitality and whimsy that characterize the best dance traditions of Mexico.

As the show progresses, love ballads give way to powerful *rancheras*, songs that were written largely by Mexican cowboys. The strength of these rousing songs finds perfect expression in the joyful voice of Ronstadt, who even brings her niece onstage to sing "Y Ándele." An old and greatly loved drinking song, "Y Ándele" is sung as a duet between Ronstadt and her niece Melinda Marie and reminds the audience that these songs are, after all, a family affair. During one of the show's many high points, a huge, cutout locomotive ferries Ronstadt and her band to center stage, and amid the sound of pistols firing into the air, they sing "Corrido de Cananea." The locomotive, a potent symbol of the Mexican revolution, withdraws once again, taking its cargo of performers with it

Ronstadt's recordings and concert performances have done much to promote awareness of the ongoing influence of Mexican culture on that of the United States. Here, she throws flowers to a crowd gathered in San Francisco, California, in 1991 to celebrate Cinco de Mayo (the fifth of May), the day when Mexicans commemorate their 1862 victory over the French conquerors of their nation.

backstage. Canciones de Mi Padre is drawing to a close.

It is hard for even the most devoted follower of Linda Ronstadt to imagine the amount of work that has gone into making this mariachi music. Clearly it is a labor of love, spurred not only by the singer's sweet family memories but also by the desire to revive a musical style on the brink of extinction. Linda Ronstadt's need to preserve these elements of Mexico's vibrant artistic history is the same quality that has made her one of the music world's most interesting and versatile performers during the past four decades.

Ronstadt reemerges onstage in yet another beautiful costume, this time a brilliantly beaded skirt that reflects the light like a thousand tiny stars. Her band stands unobtrusively off to one side as she sings "El Sol Que Tu Eres," directly to her rapt audience. Suddenly, the theater is filled with the flapping wings of dozens of white doves, released into the air as the song reaches its climax. Ronstadt stretches out her arms and two doves fly to her, resting on the fingers of each of her hands. As she finishes her song, her face lights up in a smile brighter and lovelier than anything the audience has yet witnessed. A thunderous standing ovation continues for many minutes as Ronstadt bows and yields the stage to the other musicians and dancers so they can take a bow.

Judging by the audience's emotional response, it is evident that Linda Ronstadt has accomplished what she set out to do. She has allowed her listeners to experience this stirring music just as she always has, to understand mariachi's essence, if not all the lyrics. From her modest folk music beginnings to the incredible success of Canciones de Mi Padre, Ronstadt has demonstrated that not only is singing her passion, it is also her genius.

BORDER CROSSINGS

Born in Tucson, Arizona, on July 15, 1946, Linda Marie Ronstadt seemed destined for a career in music almost from infancy. Gilbert Ronstadt, Linda's father, was himself an accomplished musician and encouraged all four of his children to listen to and learn about the music of his own childhood. He had been raised on *ranchera* and mariachi music, two popular and distinctive Mexican styles, and loved to play these songs on his guitar. Gilbert Ronstadt's grandfather had traveled to Mexico from Germany in the 1800s to seek his fortune. After serving as a soldier in the Mexican army, he became one of the first mining engineers in the northern part of the country. Soon the Ronstadt family moved even farther north from their home in the Sonora region of Mexico into Arizona, finally settling in the booming town of Tucson.

Gilbert's father loved the arid Arizona desert land and soon became a successful rancher with a large chunk of property. His side business, making parts for wagons, grew into a thriving family enterprise that eventually came to be called Ronstadt's Hardware Store. He was also a talented guitarist and singer who passed the musical traditions of Mexico down to his son Gilbert and daughter Luisa. He spent many hours

As a Mexican American, Linda Ronstadt was the inheritor of a rich musical legacy.

Ronstadt's paternal grandparents, Fred and Lupe Ronstadt (center, front and rear) with four of their children (from left), Gilbert (Linda's father), William, Edward, and Alfred.

playing and singing his favorite songs while his children listened with rapt attention. Luisa later wrote, "[I remember] those long summer evenings of my childhood, when the moon made strange patterns on my father's guitar as he sang enchanting songs to me." Gilbert Ronstadt possessed a wonderful voice that his own daughter, Linda, once described as "full of honey and thick." In his early twenties he had already enjoyed some success as a radio show singer and sometimes performed at special events. Luisa had also made a career of music, enjoying a mild stardom under the name of Luisa Espinel.

It was during these early years that Gilbert Ronstadt met his future wife, Ruthmary Copeman, an Arizona college student from a prominent Michigan family. Ruthmary's family ancestry can be traced back to the American Revolution in the United States and before that to Holland and England. Her grandfather, Lloyd Copeman, was a scientist and inventor who made his fortune by building the first version of the electric stove. Ruthmary grew up under the protective wing of her wealthy family, which fostered her sharp intelligence while sheltering her from the outside world.

While in college, Ruthmary belonged to a distinguished sorority. Legend has it that Gilbert, then a young, dashing cowboy with jet-black hair and sparkling eyes, rode his horse right up the steps of Ruthmary's sorority house to ask for a date. Soon after, they married and settled at the Ronstadt ranch in Tucson. With such circumstances, it is no surprise that Linda's singing style has often been likened to a fusion of Wild West cowgirl and shy society maiden.

Music was always Gilbert Ronstadt's true calling, but he ultimately rejected it as a career because his family did not approve. In the late 1930s, show business was considered by many to be an unsavory way to make a living. So Gilbert instead turned his attention to the family hardware store while continuing to sing and play the guitar as a hobby.

Gilbert and Ruthmary, who was often called "La" by her friends, soon had four children—Pete, the oldest; Suzi; Linda; and Mike, the youngest. They all remember with fondness the hours of music they shared with their father and how they loved to sing with him and each other. Of this time, Linda has commented, "When I was growing up, my father used

Though a talented musician in his own right, Gilbert Ronstadt devoted his life to running the family business—seen here in Tucson, Arizona, in 1905—established by his father. The Ronstadt Company was one of the largest and most prosperous family-owned businesses in the Southwest.

to play the records of Lola Beltran, the great Mexican singer, who has always been the greatest influence on my singing." Linda's brother Pete was also a strong influence on Linda's budding talent. As a member of the Tucson Boy's Choir, Pete had plenty of opportunities to show off the clear soprano voice that Linda envied so much. The purity of her brother's vocal tones provided a model for her own soprano singing long after her brother's voice changed and fell into the lower registers.

Almost before the time Linda could talk, it was clear to the family that she loved music and singing more than anything else. As she once said, "The first thing I can remember when I was a kid was just begging my father to play the guitar. I used to pester him to death." And while only a toddler, Linda found out about a magical gadget that would change her life—the radio. "I discovered how to turn on the radio when I was about three years old, and then it was all over for me," she recalls. During the long, hot Tucson summers, Linda listened to the radio stations in the area. Along with Mexican-style songs, the local stations were playing something new called rock 'n' roll that was beginning to take hold of the country.

Electrifying performers such as Elvis Presley, Chuck Berry, and Little Richard were defining a new wave of American music, and Linda was riveted to its sound. Country and western music had also become a major force, and the songs of George Jones, Tammy Wynette, and Porter Wagoner also filled the airwaves. Linda's sister, Suzi, had a particular fondness for country great Hank Williams, playing his records so often the grooves were virtually worn smooth. Since Suzi and Linda shared a bedroom, it was not surprising that the Hank Williams style became yet another potent influence. Linda was also listening to the music of Joan Baez, a singer about whom she has said, "I

In the late 1950s, as Linda Ronstadt was growing into adolescence, American popular music was being changed by a new sound—rock 'n' roll. Among its pioneers was Chuck Berry, whose distinctive songs Ronstadt heard on the radio.

thought I had a voice just like hers. Then I found out [I didn't]. The first moment you listen to yourself, it takes time to get used to that sound. It might be valid, even good, but you don't have a taste for it. . . . There weren't that many girls in Tucson who could sing that well, I guess. I just fooled myself." But rather than fooling herself, she seemed to be searching for the style that would eventually set her apart from everyone else.

Pete, Suzi, and Linda decided to form a singing trio, first called the Three Ronstadts, then the New Union Ramblers. Their youngest brother, Mike, was still a baby, so although he took part in family sings, he was too young to join his older siblings in the band. During casual practice sessions with her sister, brother, and occasionally her father, Linda always sang the high notes of a soprano. But suddenly, Linda discovered she had quite a bit more to offer. One afternoon, Suzi and Pete were practicing a song called "The Stockade Blues" by the popular folk group Peter, Paul, and Mary. As Linda tells the rest of the story, "I came walking around the corner and I threw in the high harmony. I did it in my chest voice and I surprised myself. When I started out with my chest voice, I could only sing straight, with no vibrato." All at once she realized she possessed a powerful tool that, with some training, would enable her to belt out songs just like the singers she most admired. The New Union Ramblers began to groom themselves for public appearances and were soon performing small gigs in and around Tucson.

During the 1960s, the gentle sounds of folk music became immensely popular. The Ronstadt trio's sweet young voices were perfectly suited to the difficult harmonies the style required. The Ronstadts had a flexible act in which they experimented with bluegrass music while managing to slip in some of their favorite Mexican tunes. They played wherever they could, which meant accepting gigs at a lot of coffeehouses and pizza restaurants. The group was so willing to perform that they even played at a sale event for bras and girdles. Linda had already begun taking center stage at these performances, with the blessings of her two older siblings. Suzi has said of their musical venture, "Linda had a solo spot. She sang things like 'The Trees They Do Grow High.' She was so cute and little, and she wore a black dress with a string of pearls."

Linda's memories of her Catholic education are almost uniformly terrible. As she has remembered, "I never learned anything in school. Fortunately my father taught me to read at home, but I still can't add. I had to jump into what I wanted to do right away." She had unpleasant experiences with the nuns who taught her classes. But her difficulties were not only caused by her poor performance as a student, but because Linda was also in the middle of discovering her femininity and frequently shocked the nuns by wearing tight clothing and makeup. As Linda remembered, "The nuns hated me. They hated the way I talked about boys. I was too giggly and wore too much lipstick and dressed too sexy. I came on too strong. I still do. I find myself thinking 'Oh God, red nail polish—I look like a sleaze,' or I really get into it and put on red nail polish and 500 pounds of makeup. I never know how far to go."

Even after switching to Catalina High, a nonsectarian local school, she continued her rebellious battle. As she later said, "School became irrelevant, so my choices were to sing or maybe get a job in a hotel as a waitress. I don't know how to do anything else. I feel very cheated by the system in general. . . . All I learned was how to go to sleep in class. So I don't have a high school diploma."

Although Hank Williams, the beloved Hillbilly Shakespeare, died at age 29 from "too much living," his songs—such as "Your Cheatin' Heart" and "I'm So Lonesome I Could Cry"—have lived on. Williams was a special favorite of the young Linda Ronstadt.

Luckily for Linda, a career in music seemed a clear choice right from the beginning. Shortly after she had switched to Catalina High School, Linda met Bob Kimmel, a young musician who enjoyed a reputation as an excellent guitarist. She had just turned 14 and was happy to have found a friend who was as interested in music as she was. Because Linda was already performing with her brother and sister, she seemed to eat, sleep, and breathe music. In fact, she has said of her days as a student at Catalina, "the only way I got through High School was by keeping a record player going constantly in my mind." Kimmel was impressed by the raw strength in Linda's voice and encouraged her to work hard and keep pursuing her professional ambitions. One of Linda's childhood friends, Kathryn Lance, has said that Kimmel told her, "The first time I heard Linda sing, I knew she had a voice that comes along once in a generation. I never doubted she could make it to the top." Kimmel, a little older and further along in his career, soon left for Los Angeles, but he continued to call and write in an effort to convince Linda to follow him there.

Linda, for her part, was not entirely sure she was cut out for a life so far away from her family. Although music seemed to be her brightest future prospect, she struggled with the knowledge that she would always be different as a result. Most of her friends were planning to get married and have children, while all Linda could think about doing was making records and hitting the road. Her sister, Suzi, and brothers Pete and Mike had chosen to follow fairly traditional paths after their musical act disbanded. Pete became the chief of police in Tucson, Suzi got married and settled in Arizona, and Mike decided to take over the family hardware business. After high school, Linda attempted to yield to her parents' wishes by taking courses at the University of Arizona. But after only one semester she decided to accept Bob Kimmel's offer to join him in Los Angeles and try to make it as a professional singer. Linda was now 18 years old, and the world seemed hers for the taking. She had no idea how long and rocky the road to success would be.

A DIFFERENT DRUM

Ronstadt arrived in the sun-drenched city of Los Angeles in 1964 with exactly $30 in her pocket and a $2 bill. Her father had torn off a corner of the bill for good luck and gave the bill to his daughter, while also giving her the advice, "Never let anyone take your picture with your clothes off."

The sprawling California city had become the newest mecca for young musicians eager to meet each other and experiment with the quickly changing sounds of rock 'n' roll. The music scene had begun to move south from San Francisco into the rambling vastness of the city of Los Angeles. Enclaves such as Echo Park, Laurel Canyon, and Venice were becoming home to such up-and-coming artists as Bonnie Raitt, Jackson Browne, Neil Young, Stephen Stills, and Joni Mitchell. Don Henley and Glenn Frey, two young musicians who had settled there, would soon meet and play with Linda Ronstadt, paving the way for their own success as the Eagles. Ronstadt said about that fertile time, "We were all learning about drugs, philosophy, and music. Everything was exciting."

The 1960s and early 1970s were explosive years. The youth movement was in full swing, characterized most famously by the credo "Don't trust anyone over 30." Challenging traditional attitudes had become a

In the first years of her career, Ronstadt's country-tinged sound and lovelorn ballads made her synony- mous with what came to be known as southern Califor- nia rock. The most famous performers of this style were the Eagles, seen here in one of their early incar- nations.

way of life, and old modes of behavior no longer applied. Personal freedom was highly valued, and it was believed that whatever felt good must be accept- able. Rock 'n' roll came to be a battle cry for that generation and reflected the outlook of its listeners. Popular music was intimately tied to fashion, drugs, and the sexual revolution. The songs were powerful and often full of anger; singers no longer simply sang, but screamed, growled, and wailed their lyrics, which were often about alienation and rebellion. Although sweeter than what was usually heard over the airwaves, Ronstadt's voice was well suited to the music of the times.

After staying for a time with her old friend from Arizona, Bob Kimmel, Ronstadt found herself an apartment in the Ocean Park district and was begin- ning to enjoy her independence. It was an enormous change from the protected, secure environment Tuc- son had provided, but at the age of 18 she was ready to make her own choices. One of the first things she did was to make plans to start a band. Kimmel, a good rhythm guitar player, knew of a capable lead guitarist in the area named Kenny Edwards and thought he might be the right person for their needs. Edwards and Kimmel had met in a local club called the Ash Grove, which had been attracting exciting musical acts, such as the folk/blues singer Taj Mahal and the slide guitar master Ry Cooder. Ronstadt, Kimmel, and Edwards formed a trio they called the Stone Poneys after a favorite song by the bluesman Charlie Patton called "The Stone Poney Blues."

At first the group had some difficulty deciding on a sound. Ronstadt's background had been steeped in country and western and Mexican tunes, whereas Kimmel and Edwards were both longtime folk players. When she attempted to talk about her own musical interests with the other two, Ronstadt would often meet with nothing more than two blank stares. As a result, the group was caught in an ongoing search for an identity and a sound of their own. From Ronstadt's point of view, for all their struggles they were not really successful in their attempts. As she later said, "We started off as an acoustic rock band and played clubs like the Insomniac and a lot of beer pads. . . . We had some good times and some bad times, but we were always breaking up. We were always playing in opposite musical directions. The Stone Poneys tried to combine roots with rock and roll and we were miserable."

Continuing rehearsals enabled the Stone Poneys to pull their music together, and they soon managed to land an important gig at a club called the Troubadour. The Troubadour was perhaps the most respected venue of its time, famous for showcasing new talent in shows that often led to record contracts. It was no small feat to land an engagement at the Troubadour, where established bands frequently played and heavy-hitting recording industry kingpins often sat in the audience. The Troub, as it was nicknamed, was a place where careers could be made overnight, and the Stone Poneys knew they were playing, quite literally, for high stakes.

The Stone Poneys' first performances were warmly received but did not attract much attention from music industry agents—with one notable exception. Herb Cohen, a moderately successful rock manager and promoter, had spotted the potential in Ronstadt's soaring voice. He immediately asked the manager of the club to introduce him to her. Soon Ronstadt found herself ensconced in a small bar next door to the Troub, listening to Herb Cohen talk about her future possibilities. Bob Kimmel went looking for them there later that night and, once he found them, was in for an unpleasant surprise. As Ronstadt told the story, "I remember Herbie saying to Kimmel, 'I don't know whether I can get your group a contract, but I can get your girl singer recorded,' and that was sort of the beginning. Trouble in the ranks. And I said, 'No, no, I won't sing without the group.'"

But the damage had been done, and the Stone Poneys were growing increasingly restless about working so hard and going nowhere fast. They were approached by the Troubadour's manager to do a second gig, which they welcomed as a source of potential opportunities. This time, however, things went very badly for the band. They had been scheduled to play the warmup spot for Oscar Brown, a blues and jazz guitarist who headed up his own band, and the audience's reaction to the Poneys' mellow sound was terrible. It was worse by far than being ignored, and the group was so demoralized by the experience that they broke up then and there. Ronstadt later said that they found it hard to look at one another after the show was over. She herself was so depressed by the collapse of the band that she moved to Venice, taking a break from the music scene. The rehearsal expenses had been a large drain on the band's funds, and the small gigs they had been playing before their breakup barely covered their expenses. Ronstadt had taken such a financial beating that she was forced to ask her parents for rent money. But the distance gave her time to review her options, and she finally decided to approach Herb Cohen on her own.

Their first project together was to secure Ronstadt a spot singing on a taped audition that Frank Zappa, an increasingly popular rock guitarist and composer, was making for a major record company. That fell through, however, so Cohen and Ronstadt began to toy with the possibility of reforming the Stone Poneys under Cohen's management. After they talked it over with Kimmel and Edwards, the Stone Poneys were reborn. This time Cohen fought hard to get the group heard by Nick Venet, a producer at Capitol Records. Venet had seen the group previously and had pressured Cohen to try and sign Ronstadt as a solo act. After hearing Cohen out, Venet went back to his superiors at Capitol to tell them that Ronstadt was not ready yet to perform without her band. A bargain was finally struck, and the Stone Poneys had their first major record company contract.

The Stone Poneys' first album, *Evergreen*, was a collection of mild, folk-flavored tunes. It was released in 1967 but went nowhere. The band's second effort, *Evergreen, Volume II*, was equally undistinguished and not very successful except for one song that slowly made its way up the charts. "Different Drum," a catchy, pretty tune written by Mike Nesmith, the former guitarist for the Monkees, stood out for two reasons. The first was the song itself, which gave an unusual twist to the popular love relationship theme that told the story of young woman's gentle rejection of her boyfriend. The second was the clear, ringing sound of Ronstadt's voice, which added grace and strength to the uncommon lyrics she sang. During the song's slow ascent toward success, the Stone Poneys continued to play gigs and promote their music. However, their performances were still meeting with indifference, and after a disastrous gig opening for the bluesman Paul Butterfield, the bottom fell out. The Stone Poneys broke up again, disgusted with the business and tired of not getting anywhere. This time, however, their decision to dissolve the partnership was sealed—Kenny Edwards packed his bags and moved to India.

Now, like it or not, Linda Ronstadt was on her own, but surprisingly her fortunes were changing as rapidly as the public's taste in music. "Different Drum" had by this time become a hit, and Ronstadt was getting noticed in the press. *Billboard* magazine, a publication that keeps a close eye on music industry trends, wrote in 1968, "Watch out for Linda Ronstadt."

But having a hit single was not as wonderful a feeling for Ronstadt as it should have been. After all the hard times the singer had been through with the band, the song's success left her with mixed feelings. As she has said, "Having a hit record when I was 21 made me real visible to the music community and I didn't feel I was ready for that examination. I wasn't very good and it made me real embarrassed. I felt people in the business resented me. I still struggle with that." Important music industry people were now turned expectantly in her direction and, with a third album to fulfill contractually, Ronstadt was feeling anxious.

The third album, released under the title *Linda Ronstadt: Stone Poneys and Friends*, wound up being made entirely with session musicians and cost Capitol a great deal of money. Unfortunately, sales were poor, and Ronstadt found herself financially liable to Capitol. She simply had to start making some money for the record company or be responsible for paying them back out of her own pocket. Worse, Ronstadt's fear of being able to handle the considerable pressure of controlling an audience all alone was greater than ever. As she remembered, "I was so intimidated by the quality of everybody's musicianship that instead of trying to be better, I chickened out and wouldn't work. It took me four years to get to the point where I could get on stage as a single. At first I just couldn't open my mouth on stage. I was so shy."

However, she knew it had to be done and began testing the solo waters at the Whiskey-a-Go-Go club in Los Angeles. Her appearances there also established a pattern of constantly shifting backup bands, a problem that would haunt her for years to come. The continually changing lineup of supporting musicians was blamed for the odd blandness of the following records she made for Capitol. Even though she was given some of the best session players in Los Angeles to work with, there was little cohesion to the sound. It was just not a band in the real sense, and Ronstadt's records suffered from that limited vision. It was not that the players had no talent. In fact, Ronstadt's band was often made up of the best players available, among them Glenn Frey and Don Henley, later of the Eagles. But because the players came and went, Ronstadt's music was not given a chance to grow, and her career began to falter. It seemed as though those who predicted she would be a big star were wrong.

But Ronstadt was not about to throw in the towel. She began traveling to meet and record with musicians from Nashville and Muscle Shoals, Alabama, two of the great seats of country and soul-flavored music. She was beginning to find an unusual sound that would eventually put her in a class by herself, a sound known as southern California rock. Her strong ties to country and western music and her enormous talent as a singer of ballads were leading her toward the unique style she had been searching for. Ronstadt's subsequent album, *Hand Sown . . . Home Grown*, produced in 1969, was a more accurate reflection of her new musical direction. Two songs from the album, "Silver Threads and Golden Needles," a sweet folk ballad written by the Springfields in 1962, and the Bob Dylan tune "I'll Be Your Baby Tonight" were both standouts. The record also featured songs by Randy Newman and Fred Neil, both known for their penetrating, bittersweet lyrics. Although the album was criticized for its lack of unity, it set a much higher standard for song material and offered distinct hints of the singer's future greatness.

Ronstadt's sex appeal was now being written about almost as much as the music she was making. This was both a blessing and a curse. Although it helped that her attractiveness made audiences sit up and take notice, it was also the source of much trouble in her personal life. Herb Cohen had become not only Ronstadt's manager, but also her boyfriend and, because he was quite a bit older, a kind of father figure.

The cover photograph for Ronstadt's album Silk Purse *was the first indication of her willingness to take chances with her own image.*

Her insecurities still prevented her from feeling as if she could take command of her career, and she needed Cohen's guidance. Because Ronstadt was one of the first solo female performers who could draw huge audiences, she was also blazing new trails in terms of power and control. But because of her traditional upbringing and rock 'n' roll's male-dominated milieu, she struggled with the need to be submissive and to follow other people's orders. And although her relationships with men were complex and often difficult, they also provided the emotional underpinnings of her singing. Linda Ronstadt did not just sing the songs she had chosen; she interpreted the stories they told straight from her own heart.

Ronstadt's next studio album signaled some important changes in her life and career. Called, simply, *Linda Ronstadt* and recorded in 1972, it heralded the arrival of a new producer for her material, John Boylan. The attraction between the two was immediate, and soon they were living, as well as working, together. Their close relationship was solid at first, but after a while their intimacy began to cause professional problems. As Ronstadt later remembered, "We argued a lot; we competed enormously in the studio. I just didn't trust him. I didn't trust anyone, then, and I was always afraid that something was going to get pulled over me. I was punch-drunk from producers." Nevertheless, her selection of song material was far more cohesive than it had been on her previous albums, with songs that ranged in style from Jackson Browne's folky "Rock Me on the Water" to "I Still Miss Someone," by country singer Johnny Cash. And like Ronstadt's earlier albums, a new backup group had been assembled, including the highly talented drummer Don Henley and guitarist Glenn Frey.

Although Ronstadt faced many difficulties working with Boylan, he was also the producer for her next album, released in 1973, called *Don't Cry Now.* The big difference this time lay in her switch from Capitol Records to Asylum, an up-and-coming label with a high-profile executive and talent finder named David Geffen calling the shots. Geffen had been responsible for discovering and developing some of the biggest musical talent in the industry and was fast on his way to becoming the richest man in the record business. *Don't Cry Now* was much more successful than Ronstadt's previous albums, due in part to Geffen's reputation for excellence and his genius for promotion. But the production of *Don't Cry Now* had been rocky from the start and had caused a tremendous amount of tension for everyone involved. Ronstadt's faith in her ability was at an all-time low, and she spent much of the recording time so depressed that she would simply put her head down on the consoles and fall asleep. From her vantage point, anything was better than having to complete the tasks at hand. She hated the way the album was sounding and despaired of finding any way to make it better. But like the cavalry that shows up just in the nick of time, Peter Asher was pulled into production during the final sessions for *Don't Cry Now.* Asher, a former musician and very successful producer, did his best to pull the album out of its doldrums.

But by this time, Ronstadt had also met John David Souther, a songwriter, musician, and producer whom she has called the great love of her life. Souther swept her off her feet and out of the house of John Boylan, where she had been living for some time. Souther's hand was also the final one on the production of *Don't Cry Now.* Although Asher's input had been welcome, working on a project so late in its development had not been entirely satisfying. Too much of the album was already out of Asher's control, and Ronstadt had been too insecure to bring him in

While making the album Don't Cry Now, *Ronstadt fell hard for the charismatic country-rocker J. D. Souther. Some have interpreted her vocals on the hit single "Faithless Love" as commentary on her experience with the wandering Souther.*

until the very end. Instead, Ronstadt and Souther rerecorded all the songs on the album by themselves. As Ronstadt remembered, "We were like kids in the studio, just inept, and we took a lot of time. But I learned a lot and it was worth it, almost, because it was such hard work. After that experience, I knew so much more when I went into the studio."

The album as a whole displayed the various production inconsistencies, but it also demonstrated Ronstadt's growing vocal range. She was getting closer to finding the depth of her own abilities even though she rejected outright the idea of writing her own song material. As she said about the process, "It's a real problem for me to make albums. I don't write songs."

Although her gear-shifting in love affairs may have seemed rather sudden to outsiders, Ronstadt had actually become more circumspect about her romances. She later said that mixing business and sex "is always a bad idea." Boylan was still her producer during this very complex and emotional time, but another long-time relationship was coming to an end. Herb Cohen, who had continued to be Ronstadt's manager well after any personal entanglement had ended, had been asked to relinquish his position. The management change cost Ronstadt a great deal of money because she was forced to continue paying Cohen commissions, but she wanted the freedom to make some necessary changes. Her own ideas about music were becoming bolder, and, in the breathtaking rush that had always characterized her speech, she was expressing them. Suddenly, Linda Ronstadt's management decisions were in her own hands, and things were looking a lot brighter.

HEART LIKE A WHEEL

*D*on't Cry Now remained on the charts for almost 45 weeks. It had become clear to Ronstadt and those close to her that the album's success was to a large degree attributed to Peter Asher's hand in its production. In the short period of time Asher worked with Ronstadt, her confidence and optimism had become stronger than ever. The only hitch in making their collaboration a permanent arrangement was the timing. Asher already had his hands full with several projects, and, much as he respected Ronstadt's voice and potential, he could not honorably break his other commitments.

It was this sense of honor and loyalty that Ronstadt found so refreshing, as well as Asher's ability to get her to relax during recording sessions and allow her emotions to shine through a song. Peter Asher was no stranger to technique, having started out in England in 1962 as one half of the soft-rock act Peter and Gordon. The duo had two radio hits, "Lady Godiva" and "World Without Love," written by John Lennon and Paul McCartney. But in 1967, when no other musical successes seemed to be in the cards, Peter and Gordon went their separate ways. This suited Asher just fine

Though her emerging status as sex symbol and chart-topping commercial success did not immediately ease all Ronstadt's artistic insecurities, she grew steadily more confident as a performer during the 1970s.

43

because he had always preferred working backstage to being front and center. His true talents lay in the production end of the business, and he was possessed of that rare ability to focus his attention utterly on another artist.

Years before, Peter and his sister Jane had been child film stars. More recently, Jane had achieved a different kind of notoriety by being the very serious girlfriend of Beatle Paul McCartney. McCartney soon approached Peter, who had gone back to London University as a philosophy major, to ask him to join the Apple Records label as a talent scout. He agreed and went on to discover and sign the singer and guitarist James Taylor to his first major contract. Asher also agreed to represent James Taylor's sister, Kate, and his work for her was a major obstacle in handling Linda Ronstadt at the same time. Asher felt that not only would it have been a conflict of interest, but he preferred to devote himself exclusively to only a few clients.

Asher's success with James Taylor, building the musician's career up from a cult following to major stardom with the *Sweet Baby James* release, made him highly desirable as a manager and producer. Perhaps it was fortunate that, as luck would have it, Ronstadt was in no position to think too much about Asher. Two days after finishing *Don't Cry Now*, Ronstadt and her band of session men hit the road for a three-and-a-half-month tour opening for rocker Neil Young.

Touring was never easy for Ronstadt and harder still when playing in the shadows of a more popular band. Neil Young's stardom was at the first of many peaks, and audiences were coming to see him—not a petite, country-flavored brunette in cutoff denim shorts. The fact that she had been added to the bill after the tour was sold out made matters worse. Audiences were not expecting her, and the crowds were often restless and impatient. To alleviate some of the pressure, Ronstadt began using drugs and found herself falling into self-destructive habits. As she said, "You have to face 20,000 people, and you can't just write off St. Louis because you're feeling low." Her need for stimulants was leading her into a cocaine habit that would cause her to have her sinuses cauterized twice due to bleeding. Ronstadt had never been a drinker, but she knew she was headed for problems if she did not find another way to allay her tension.

Ronstadt was also speaking to Boylan, who was now acting as her manager, many times a day and was confused about their future together. As she has said of their relationship, "He started out to be my boyfriend, then he was managing me and producing me. Then he wasn't producing me but he was still managing me, and then he wasn't managing me anymore. All those troubles stem from the fact that in our personal relationship, we couldn't resolve things." But some positive things also came out of the tour with Young. For one thing, Ronstadt had begun to play an acoustic guitar onstage, which gave her a much greater sense of confidence and comfort. She was also learning through adversity to take greater command of her backup band—to learn how to call the shots and communicate better. Playing a guitar helped enormously when it came to telling her band how she wanted certain songs to sound. Although touring was certainly no picnic, it provided the push Ronstadt needed to help find her strength as the artistic center of a musical group.

Another piece of good luck was Ronstadt's chance meeting with Kate Taylor after a show one night. Kate told her that Asher was no longer working for her and that he might be free to take on a new client. This was terrific news for Ronstadt, who felt more than ever that she needed the stability Peter Asher offered as a manager and producer. She called Asher immediately, and the deal was on its way to being done. Linda Ronstadt's partnership with Peter Asher would not only turn out to be a platinum musical combination but would even radically change the way Ronstadt perceived herself. Clearly, Ronstadt desperately needed Asher's innate sensibility about what was right in her music. She had been having trouble finding her direction through the morass of personal difficulties with her managers and producers. As Ronstadt explained it, "If you are living with someone who is also in the music business, it's bound to cause resentment. There's no way around it. . . . If he is more talented than I am, that makes me nervous. If I'm more successful than he is, that makes him nervous."

In Asher, Ronstadt finally found the objectivity she needed. His opinion was never colored by events that took place outside the studio. Asher's respect for Ronstadt's ideas and talent also had the much-needed effect of rubbing off on the performer herself. Ronstadt's singing began to reflect her growing self-reliance, and she started taking better care of herself in general. She took up jogging when she was not touring and was amazed by how much fitter she felt in both body and mind. As she says, "People have different ways of coping with their situations so they won't be completely driven under by the pressure and the strain of bad food and a weird, irregular life-style. My way is running. It absolutely works for me as a depression cure and as a health helper."

The fact that there was never any question of a romance between manager and star was also a big help in establishing a supportive professional relationship. Peter Asher was happily married, and his wife, Betsy, was becoming a close friend of Ronstadt's. Because the troublesome issue of romance had been avoided altogether, Ronstadt could get down to the business of making beautiful music. In speaking of Asher, Ronstadt positively glowed with admiration when she told an interviewer, "Peter Asher was the first person who ever discovered that I could speak English, or had an intellect." In addition, Asher never made her feel helpless or needy the way so many of her manager-boyfriends had in the past. About her previous experiences she says, "The more they encouraged me to be stupid and act silly, the more I would be dependent on them, and the more power they would have. But that was my fault. I allowed it to happen, so I'm not putting the blame for that on anybody but myself."

Asher and Ronstadt's studio alliance also brought about a change in Ronstadt's ability to treat making music like a real business to be worked on and developed. Prior to Asher's influence, Ronstadt's behavior and disposition had been helter-skelter during her recording sessions. Never known for being punctual, Ronstadt was often so late arriving at the recording studio that she would be forced to lay down tracks in a hurry. As a result of the time crush, she would feel out of control and unsatisfied with the final product. Asher's arrival on the scene helped Ronstadt accomplish more during her time in the studio. But it was not only Asher's ability to establish a sense of order that helped so much. Also crucial was the way he involved Ronstadt as a partner in the musical and business decisions that needed to be made. As she says, "Peter was the first person willing to work with me as an equal, even though his abilities were far superior to mine. I didn't have to fight for my ideas. . . . All of a sudden, making records became so much more fun."

Ronstadt's new attitude was evident in the quality of her singing. Always the first to be self-effacing, even

Ronstadt had to admit that her voice was sounding great. It certainly seemed as if coming up with new ideas for song material and taking a few risks was paying off. But, as Ronstadt has pointed out, a lot of the improvements came directly as the result of her work with Asher: "I'm a mirror. A real reflective person, and in a way it's horrible because I'm always at the mercy of my surroundings. So I need a catalyst, always, and I need a good sounding board that I can trust."

Ronstadt also knew that she had found a producer who would not, as she says, "grease" her or tell her something sounded good when it did not. She needed to hear honestly when an approach was wrong or that something was going to be difficult to accomplish. Asher's sincerity translated directly into encouragement for Ronstadt, and she found herself thinking harder than she ever had about her career. Asher's strategy was to attack any problems that arose with directness, finding good solutions rather than whitewashing the obstacles they encountered. This led to the healthiest kind of dependence a musician can have with a producer; put simply, total faith in his or her judgment. As Ronstadt has said, "I can't imagine working with someone else. There are things that he has to tolerate about me—my insecurities, I'm disorganized, I'm late or whatever. . . . We have developed tolerance in the sterling sense of the word for each other's faults, and sometimes we get angry at each other, but we pass over it. It's like a marriage."

Whereas the role of a manager is fairly easy to imagine, what exactly is a producer's function? Like any job that involves overseeing a lot of different details, a producer is first and foremost an organizer of people and events. A producer must help select the music, work on the arrangements, and choose the right session musicians or fine-tune an already existing band. All these efforts must take place before studio recording begins, and it is a tremendous job for one person. But being organized was the foundation of Peter Asher's reputation; that and taking the time to make sure everything was absolutely right, no matter what the cost. The results were immediately apparent, and Ronstadt lavishly praised Asher's approach: "Everybody always knows exactly what's expected of them, and they try to do it the best they can. If they get off the track, he's real precise about guiding you back. . . . The sessions are really well-organized and

Unsure of her own artistic judgment, in the early years of her career Ronstadt relied heavily on producers to shape her sound, often with unfortunate results. In Peter Asher (left), Ronstadt found, for the first time, a producer with whom she felt comfortable both musically and personally, and the result was her first great commercial and critical success, the album Heart Like a Wheel.

well-run, and I find it's like that notion—from the most discipline comes the most freedom. It just seems that when you provide a real strong framework like that, then everybody has the confidence to do their best." With Asher's help, Linda Ronstadt was growing up, getting stronger, and gearing up for the first smash album of her career.

Heart Like a Wheel, the 1974 album that exploded onto the charts immediately after its release, was a marvelous consummation of Asher and Ronstadt's first experience working together from start to finish. Although Ronstadt had decided to record on the Asylum label, this album was created for Capitol due to her previous contract commitments. The music, a deft combination of the mellow southern California sound and Ronstadt's own country-style roots, forged a new union between pop and country. It also started a trend by many famous country and western singers, including Dolly Parton, Emmylou Harris, and Glen Campbell, to make crossover albums of their own.

Among the hit singles from *Heart Like a Wheel* that dominated the airwaves was one of Ronstadt's most plaintive yet powerful offerings, "When Will I Be Loved." Written by Phil Everly of the Everly Brothers, the song became a pop standard. More than being a complaint about what is lacking, "When Will I Be Loved" sounds like a demand for love that is rightfully due. The forceful, propulsive music under-scores lyrics that seem to convey that being a victim is out of the question; the way Ronstadt sings the song, there can be no doubt that the sentiment is close to her own heart.

The album received tremendous critical praise, and, with the help of three more radio hits, "You're No Good," "I Can't Help It If I'm Still in Love with You," and "Faithless Love," *Heart Like a Wheel* be-came the number one album on the charts. Another

The multitalented Andrew Gold was responsible for much of the success of Heart Like a Wheel, *but his solo career never caught fire after he left Ronstadt's band.*

contributing factor to the monster success of the album was versatile musician Andrew Gold, who received special credit for assisting with the musical arrangements. His influence can be heard on almost every song, as can his playing of the piano, acoustic and electric guitar, and even percussion. Gold's virtuoso style was also flexible enough to adapt to the changing moods of the songs on *Heart Like a Wheel*, and he has sometimes been credited with having as much control over the album as Asher. Unquestion-

ably, the combination of Asher, Ronstadt, and Gold
was a winner; the album sold over a million copies and
made Ronstadt not only a household word but a
commercial force in the music industry.

Strangely enough, Ronstadt's musical triumph
with *Heart Like a Wheel* had some unpleasant effects
on the feelings of the brand-new star. The insecurity
and uncertainty she had always fought against pushed
their way to the surface, leaving her depressed and
uneasy. She assessed her emotional state during that
time in this way: "The first thing I had to do when
Heart Like a Wheel went platinum was stop feeling
guilty about my success. The most miserable time of
my life was in 1975, after the album. All of my dreams
of success had come true, but I still felt like the same
old schlep. I was still feeling very untrustworthy. Now
I realize that I worked hard and earned my success,
and it's up to me whether I enjoy it or not." It was
extremely difficult for Ronstadt to make the transi-
tion from being a shy, vulnerable girl singer to feeling
comfortable as a major star whose record sales left no
doubt as to her appeal. She had come a very long way
indeed from playing pizza joints and beer dives, and
the adjustment was tough for the young woman who
still questioned the quality of her own gift.

Ronstadt's listening public, however, never
doubted that she was indeed the real thing, and *Heart
Like a Wheel* soon garnered her first Grammy Award.
Coincidentally, it was a song called "I Can't Help It,"
written by Ronstadt's childhood favorite, Hank Williams, that enabled her to join the stellar ranks of
Grammy winners. It was fitting also that Ronstadt
should win her first Grammy for Best Female
Country Vocal Performance. After all, she had always
considered country music her true stylistic base and
was proud to be able to incorporate it into the larger
format   of   pop-rock.   Most   astonishing   about

Ronstadt's win, however, was the competition she overcame when she was selected by the awards panel. Dolly Parton, the veritable queen of country and western music, was knocked out of the race by dark-horse Ronstadt, a relative neophyte in the category. It must have caused Ronstadt no small anguish to have been chosen over the country singer she most admired as a talent and as a person, but the verdict was in. Ronstadt was an acknowledged star.

LINDA IN DISGUISE

As the media grabbed hold of its newest female pop icon, Linda Ronstadt began to confront the trials and terrors of life in the limelight. The unbridled success of *Heart Like a Wheel* had also led to an increased touring schedule for Ronstadt, keeping her on the road for months at a time. Although she was slowly becoming more comfortable onstage singing to huge audiences, she was ambivalent about performing and found it very difficult to cope with the demands of touring.

Ronstadt has always fought hard to maintain her sense of self, but it has not always been easy. She had struggled with the idea that she was not beautiful since childhood, and being in the public eye only made those feelings worse. As she said, "I get pimples and I get fat easily, and my nose is too thick. You can never look as good in real life as your album covers. It makes me testy sometimes dealing with strangers and all their expectations. Carly [Simon] won't perform—she has stage fright—and I just barely do it. It's unnatural. Your sense of identity is reflected back to you in an amazingly distorted way."

With time, she has become more relaxed about her physical appearance and usually feels liberated enough to dress accordingly. Her popularity un-

With the success of Heart Like a Wheel, *which reached number one on the album charts and yielded four hit singles, Ronstadt became the most popular female vocalist in the United States.*

Despite her success as a recording artist, Ronstadt remained a shy onstage performer, although she grew steadily more comfortable in front of an audience as her career progressed.

deniably increased on a scale with the delight fans took in her camisole and high-heel outfits. The sense of innocent vulnerability she gives off is appealing to both sexes, in that men feel protective and women identify with her. Somehow, Ronstadt's attitudes have always been palpable to her audience, striking a deep chord of responsiveness in the crowd for the sweet-faced woman onstage who sings bravely through her fear.

The real Ronstadt is revealed most clearly in the songs she chooses to perform. She has always refused to sing material that does not feel close to her in some intrinsic way, and a song must have personal resonance before it makes its way into her repertoire. As she has said, "Though the melody has to match up to what I can do, the lyrics are the main thing. I look for something that feels like it's about me. Just like a songwriter will write a song that is about some feeling he just went through. I can't really sing a song that doesn't express my feelings in some way." Her sincerity during performances, although it has made for erratic swings in the energy and mood of her shows, is refreshing.

Presenting an honest face instead of a showbiz mask is a choice Ronstadt has made very consciously. As she once commented, "I'm never a different person offstage than I am onstage. I don't have a stage personality." Her fans are not only more loyal as a result, but also very patient when Ronstadt's discomfort manifests itself during a performance. The crowd becomes supportive rather than restless, giving the singer loud encouragement when her shyness threatens to overwhelm her. Not many singers are able to engender this kind of unconditional devotion. Yet Ronstadt continued to have trouble facing even the most accepting of fans for reasons that she made clear when she told an interviewer, "Being on stage is like being at a cocktail party with a bunch of people that you don't know and nobody gets to talk but you. You have to carry the whole conversation." Being the focal point of people's attention is, ironically, a painful experience for Ronstadt, whose stardom has made it impossible to escape the spotlight.

An important mainstay for Ronstadt over the years has been her close relationships with the women she has met in and out of the music business. She has even formed durable and supportive friendships with women who might ordinarily be considered her rivals. Emmylou Harris has been a longtime confidante, even though Ronstadt once confessed to being absolutely terrified of meeting her. "Everyone was telling me for two years that there was this girl who was doing everything that I was doing, and they were raving about her. I felt threatened by it. I was afraid. I was afraid to meet her. I thought, 'Oh, no, what if she's better than I am?' Then I met her and she was. I feel that she is the best country-rock person. I'm moving in more of a pop direction anyway. And I was

stunned because I had been doing this for a long time and I knew exactly how her talents compared to mine. I also loved her immediately when I met her, because she's honest and she's nice. There was no way I couldn't like her."

Ronstadt's friendship with Harris came at an excellent time, right on the heels of the completion of the album *Don't Cry Now*. As Ronstadt said, "I had just broken up with someone I was living with. The relationship had been real oppressive to me. It lasted a long time and created a lot of fear in my music. He was a musician, too. After we broke up, I seemed to make a lot of friends all of a sudden. I met Emmylou Harris in Washington and she turned me on to a lot of people." Ronstadt was gaining strength through her friendships with women, many of whom were also single. This solidarity led reporters to ask why she wasn't a more outspoken supporter of women's rights. As she said, "Sometimes people ask me why I'm not a feminist and that's really crazy. You see, obviously I am, because I'm an independent woman; I have been since I was eighteen. I earn my own living. I'm dependent on no man. I'm a free agent."

Ronstadt's lack of competitiveness with women has always been a far cry from the feelings she battled in her relationships with men. With female friendships, her nurturing side takes over and has won her the loyalty of many girlfriends, among them Bonnie Raitt, Dolly Parton, Phoebe Snow, and songwriters Karla Bonoff and Wendy Waldman. Whenever she could, Ronstadt tried to incorporate their work on her albums by way of lending professional support. Emmylou Harris's sweet voice can be heard frequently as a backup vocalist on Ronstadt's albums, and Bonoff and Waldman have contributed songs. Another woman with whom Ronstadt feels especially close is Maria Muldaur, a raven-haired singer most famous for her hit "Midnight at the Oasis" in the 1970s.

Although she never attained Ronstadt's fame as a performer in her own right, Karla Bonoff penned many of Ronstadt's best-known songs.

Ronstadt has cited their friendship as a strong influence in encouraging her growing sense of self-
assurance. As she said, "I really feel I was justified in
not feeling confident until now. Now I don't have any
excuse except for myself. In lots of ways, Maria and
I have had parallel lives—similar careers, similar relationships with men, similar problems. Now we lend
each other clothes, and we bolster each other."

Ronstadt's next album, after the wild success of
Heart Like a Wheel and a 1974 re-release of some old
Capitol recordings under the title *Different Drum*, was
Prisoner in Disguise. Completed in 1975, *Prisoner in
Disguise* showcased Ronstadt's diversity in a way her
other albums had only hinted at. Her choice of song
material was more varied in style and mood, ranging
from the stately Neil Young tune "Love Is Like a
Rose" to a rave rendition of "Heat Wave," a song
Martha and the Vandellas made famous in the early
1960s. Between these vocal polar opposites lay
"Tracks of My Tears," a Smokey Robinson offering
that became a big radio hit, and Jimmy Cliff's soulful
"Many Rivers To Cross." Other tunes on the album
came from Ronstadt's favorite stock of songwriters,
including Anna McGarrigle, who wrote the lovely
title song from *Heart Like a Wheel*, James Taylor, J. D.
Souther, and Lowell George. Although the record did
not gain the same startling tour de force status that
Heart Like a Wheel acquired, it nonetheless moved up
the charts swiftly and soon went gold.

Ronstadt's backup band was also beginning to
take shape, and the roster had been steadier for each
successive album. Andrew Gold, who would leave
before Ronstadt's next album to pursue a solo career,
again contributed to the arrangements and overall
musical excellence of *Prisoner in Disguise*. The guitarist
Waddy Wachtel and Kenny Edwards, her former
bandmate from the Stone Poneys, were also becoming

regulars during recording sessions, as well as on the road. This contributed to a growing sense of unity in Ronstadt's music and a better onstage rapport when playing to a crowd. Rock critic Robert Christgau pointed out that *Prisoner in Disguise* presented an interesting problem for Ronstadt. Because her specialty had become covering really fine song material, rather than singing mediocre songs and getting by on the sheer force of her personality, she faced a dilemma. The songs she chose were often classics that required her to reach higher than perfection in order to measure up to their previous renditions. It was hard to compete with Smokey Robinson singing "Tracks of My Tears," but not impossible; it just had to be performed in exactly the right way. Happily for music history, the team that Asher and Ronstadt had assembled was up to the task.

After *Prisoner in Disguise* came the 1976 album *Hasten down the Wind*. Although Ronstadt admits that she was "very depressed" during the making of this album, it managed to go platinum in just a few weeks. It also garnered her a second Grammy and secured her position as rock's foremost female star. It is true that the songs were more consistently downbeat than those found on her previous two records, but her energetic cover of Buddy Holly's "That'll Be the Day" was soon a radio standard. Ronstadt had also decided to stray from her usual songwriting crew in favor of trying a few new artists. John and Johanna Hall, Tracy Nelson, and Ry Cooder were all featured, as was an offering by Karla Bonoff entitled "Someone To Lay Down Beside Me." Most exciting was the addition of a tune called "Lo Siento Mi Vida," a Mexican-flavored song written by Ronstadt's father, Gilbert, and guitarist Kenny Edwards.

Ronstadt herself wrote a song for the album, one called "Try Me Again." She was heard to complain that the song was so confessional she was embarrassed to even sing it. As she said of her unusual foray into songwriting, "Some people sit down every day to write, but I don't do that. I have a few ideas cooking, but my goal in life is not to be a songwriter. The fact that I wrote a song was like an added bonus in my life. But something pretty intense has to happen and it's got to be something I can write about in pretty specific terms. The whole combination of events has to happen in order for me to write a song. I just don't have the kind of craftsmanship that a writer would have to have to construct things out of everyday experiences, in a way that makes it real interesting. Paul Simon is the most gifted at that. He can write songs outside of his own experience so eloquently."

The 20th anniversary of the Grammys saw Ronstadt much more prepared for her win. Songwriter Paul Williams and the former Beatles drummer Ringo Starr presented Ronstadt with her award. Although her win in the country and western category had been wonderful on a personal level, the award for Best Pop Vocal was far more important. It was the most sought-after category by both male and female performers due to the tremendous publicity it generated for the honorees. Taking the top pop honors also meant becoming firmly established in the pop-rock pantheon. Ronstadt accepted her award with shy words of thanks, wearing a pale, off-the-shoulder gown and her dark hair piled high. By winning her second grammy, Ronstadt joined the ranks of such music industry legends as Judy Garland, Barbra Streisand, and Dionne Warwick. Was it any wonder that a legion of critics were beginning to think that Linda Ronstadt could do no wrong?

Also in 1976, Ronstadt was voted Top Female Singer by the readers of *Playboy* magazine in both the Pop and Country categories. The poll was a favorite among industry watchdogs, as *Playboy* was one of the decade's most influential and widely read publications. Soon after, Asylum released the album *Linda Ronstadt's Greatest Hits*.

The following year, after winning the *Playboy* poll in both categories for a second year running, the singer made another big splash with an album of new material, called *Simple Dreams*. Interestingly enough, Ronstadt's latest offering was as bright and sunny as *Hasten down the Wind* had been gloomy and somber. She once commented that much of the first side of *Simple Dreams* can be considered autobiographical in subject matter. Certainly one of the big hits from the record, Buddy Holly's "It's So Easy," spelled out Ronstadt's ongoing trials and tribulations in matters of the heart. As she has said, "When you're a teenager or in your early twenties, romance is the whole thing. . . . If you weren't in love, you pretended you were. Then all the problems came . . . the fights, the breakups. Love didn't turn out to be so easy after all. There were always scars." But for all the trouble it seemed clear that Ronstadt had never been in such fine voice or more in control of her musical direction.

Simple Dreams combined the best of a few different worlds. Although two standards stood out front and center—"It's So Easy" and Roy Orbison's "Blue Bayou"—there was also a deft remake of the Rolling Stones' hard-rocking "Tumbling Dice." Balancing these pure rock offerings were gentle ballads such as the country standard "Old Paint" and "I Never Will Marry," a song written by the country singer Dolly Parton, who also sang it as a duet with Ronstadt. Warren Zevon, who later scored big with his humorous song "Werewolves of London," contributed two songs, "Carmelita" and a comic plaint called "Poor, Poor Pitiful Me." Moving ballads by J. D. Souther, Waddy Wachtel, and Eric Kaz were chosen to round

For Ronstadt, one of the drawbacks to her immense stardom during the 1970s was that her personal life became a subject of as much interest to fans and the media as her music. Besides J. D. Souther, she was linked romantically during that time with Mick Jagger, lead singer of the Rolling Stones, and Jerry Brown, governor of California.

out an album of surprising diversity. Although Andrew Gold had moved on to his own projects, there was little lost in the way of quality, which fed Ronstadt's growing sense of accomplishment. Gold had been more or less the leader of the band, but his style was beginning to seem too forced and clever for the laid-back charm of Ronstadt's material. Because he already had a top 10 hit on the radio with a song called

"Lonely Boy," it seemed a perfect time for Gold to make his own way in the music world.

The inclusion of "Tumbling Dice" on *Simple Dreams* was rather startling for Ronstadt's older fans, who were used to her softer approach to music. In fact, it had been the suggestion of Rolling Stone Mick Jagger that Ronstadt cover the song. As the story goes, Jagger came backstage after a London show Ronstadt had given and told her she should be doing more rock 'n' roll. Jagger felt her voice packed the necessary wallop to deliver a rock message and urged her to explore the style more fully. It seemed only fair that Ronstadt should choose "Tumbling Dice" as her first rock cover and that Jagger would act as her personal coach while she was staying in London.

As a whole, *Simple Dreams*, with its selection of great songs honestly expressed, won over an entirely new flock of fans. Ronstadt herself said about the album, "I think *Simple Dreams* is a great statement about California music." And critics who had, in the past, claimed to be annoyed by Ronstadt's ongoing dialogue with heartbreak, finally seemed to see the light. As Susan Lydon wrote about the album, "Every single woman I knew, even the most hardcore feminist, experienced the same emotional needs, and with precisely the same passionate intensity that Linda's soaring, searing soprano expressed so acutely . . . . There was Linda Ronstadt blowing the whole game by singing about my forbidden feelings for millions of people, talking about them in print, gaining in popularity with every fresh heartbreak." The combination of Asher's clear, smooth production and the more homespun instincts of Ronstadt's country-rooted music was as compelling as it had ever been.

THE PIRATE QUEEN

In the role of Mabel, Ronstadt reaches for a high note in the New York Shakespeare Festival's production of Gilbert and Sullivan's Pirates of Penzance, *which was staged in Central Park in the summer of 1979. At the time, Ronstadt's performance was considered a radical change of pace for her career; it foreshadowed even more daring departures to come.*

Ronstadt released two more albums in 1977—Asylum's *Blue Bayou*, a compilation of previously issued material, and a Capitol collection called *Retrospective*. The latter became a popular seller, incorporating five tracks from *Heart Like a Wheel* and six from *Linda Ronstadt*. Both Capitol and Asylum were eager to capitalize on Ronstadt's popularity and knew the time was right for pushing her music.

As the 1970s drew to a close, Ronstadt was looking fitter than ever and beginning to streamline a newer image. Her next album, 1978's *Living in the U.S.A.*, was sassier and hipper than her previous offerings, highlighting the singer's new upbeat mood. The album's cover epitomized the change in Ronstadt, featuring her looking slim and sexy in a satin bomber jacket and wearing a pair of roller skates. *Living in the U.S.A.* also offered the most interesting material Ronstadt had ever assembled—including songs by Elvis Presley, Elvis Costello, Warren Zevon, and the band Little Feat—and one song from the album, "Just One Look," was one of the year's top radio hits.

Another interesting development in Ronstadt's career was her first film appearance, which came in the rock-oriented movie *FM*. A boisterous comedy about wheeling and dealing at a Los Angeles radio station

Ronstadt relaxes with costar Michael Brandon after a successful take on the set of the film FM, *in which she played herself performing in concert.*

called QSKY, the movie's plot was simplistic and seemed little more than an excuse to showcase some good rock 'n' roll, but it was a chance for Linda to take a turn on the big screen. She appears in the film in concert and sings three of her popular favorites—"Tumbling Dice," "Poor, Poor Pitiful Me," and Elvis Presley's ballad "Love Me Tender." *FM* did gain some attention for Ronstadt's performance, as well as for the performances of Eileen Brennan, Martin Mull, and Alex Karras.

At the same time, something else had been occupying a great deal of Ronstadt's attention and had caused her to become more than a little irritated with the press. In 1978, terrible storms in Los Angeles had caused severe flooding and the danger of tremendous coastal damage, especially in places like Malibu. The public was surprised to read that California governor Jerry Brown had alerted the National Guard to begin sandbagging houses along that stretch of beach. One of the first houses they were directed to belonged to Linda Ronstadt. In the tabloids, it was suggested that Ronstadt was receiving special treatment from the state government because of her personal relationship with the governor.

Ronstadt and Brown first met in 1976 when Ronstadt sang at a Democratic party fund-raiser. Sometime later, the two were formally introduced in a Los Angeles Mexican eatery called Lucy's El Adobe. The owners, Frank and Lucy Casada, knew both Brown and Ronstadt as steady customers and had decided to try their hands at a little matchmaking. The pair hit it off and from that meeting became intimate friends, while having to dodge a fascinated press corps every step of the way. Jerry Brown was thought to be a strong contender for the Presidential nomination in 1980, and the public was eager to follow the progress of the pop star and the politician.

A heavily publicized trip to Africa put the relationship between Brown and Ronstadt squarely in the spotlight, as did the humorous *Rolling Stone*

In the late 1970s and early 1980s, Ronstadt's most frequent male companion was Governor Jerry Brown of California.

magazine poll that gave Brown the "Groupie of the Year" award. But beyond the fuel it gave to gossip reporters, the friendship between Brown and Ronstadt was sincere and seemed as if it might even become serious. Ronstadt had been taking some time away from the decade-long rigors of her touring and recording schedules to be with Brown. And her name had been connected to the White House more than once during the Carter administration. Ronstadt was certainly not out of her league in the political arena, but as her mother, Ruthmary, commented, "I know she would not like being a political wife." Marriage, as Ronstadt has always said, did not top her list of desires, and she had a good time with Brown, who shared many of her interests, without it being an issue. They only began to drift away from one another, as politics began to weigh more heavily on Brown and Ronstadt again felt the itch to create new music.

The ongoing question for Ronstadt now was, what can a rock 'n' roll legend do to top her previous achievements? Ronstadt was fast moving into the 1980s and the prime of her adulthood. At age 34, her own tastes were changing, as were those of her maturing fans, and it was getting harder to decide which direction to pursue. As a single career woman, Ronstadt also felt the press of time as the possibilities of marriage and children seemed as remote as ever. As she told a reporter, "The price I pay for my life-style is not being able to have domesticity. Domestic bliss must be the highest form of bliss a human being can experience. I have profound respect for it. A woman who can do all it involves and have a career is really the exception." Nevertheless, she looked forward to becoming older and more mature, knowing that it would bring a greater sense of feeling in command of her destiny.

In 1979, Ronstadt met the highly acclaimed producer/director Joseph Papp on one of her visits to New York City, a place she was soon to make her home base. Ronstadt had heard about his work with the Public Theater and liked him right away. During that initial meeting, Ronstadt mentioned that she was intrigued with the idea of pursuing a more theatrical direction in her career. Ronstadt's appearance in the movie *FM* had given her a taste of moviemaking, and she was interested in sampling the theater as yet another venue. Even though the only Broadway drama Ronstadt had seen recently had been the play *Equus*, she knew she was interested in experimenting with drama. Her fondness for the novel *La Vagabonde*, by the French writer Colette, had also stirred up some provocative thoughts about acting. Ronstadt became fascinated with the possibilities for, as she put it, "an act where theater and music and intimacy are blended."

Ronstadt pets a camel during a 1979 trip to the African nation of Kenya. Her celebrity status has enabled Ronstadt to see much of the world.

Later in the winter of the same year, Papp called Ronstadt with an earnest invitation to appear in his new production of Gilbert and Sullivan's *Pirates of Penzance*. Papp's theater company, the New York

Shakespeare Festival, planned to bring the Gilbert and Sullivan operetta to Central Park on July 15 the following year. The piece had been chosen in honor of the 100th anniversary of the creation of *Pirates* by the British musical duo. Their productions had been hugely popular with English audiences and had become legendary among performers for being tricky and difficult to sing. The style, in which words were crowded into slippery tunes that seemed nearly impossible to follow, set a new standard for comic opera in English. Added to the singing was the necessity for good acting because, after all, Gilbert and Sullivan was musical theater, not just song recitations. *Pirates of Penzance* incorporated the most daunting elements of Gilbert and Sullivan's best work. Ronstadt later admitted she was nervous about accepting the role, mostly because she was afraid Papp would not take her seriously. As she said, "The stereotype is that New York theater people . . . think California is a fairy world full of Lotus eaters and cuckoo brains. But we had a real good rapport. When he called me with this idea I just said, 'You bet.'"

Ronstadt was so excited about Papp's offer that she immediately canceled an upcoming summer concert tour that would have brought her more than $1 million in profits. Instead, she accepted the challenging part of Mabel in *Pirates of Penzance* for the relatively trifling sum of $400 a week. She was finally confident enough in her own success to feel as though this foray into a new area would not involve much long-term risk. As she put it, "Even if I fall on my face with this, I'm sure I'll still be able to do records and concerts. So it's sort of an adventure, a holiday with lots of support." But Ronstadt also knew that taking on the role would force her to push the limits of her vocal range and explore a new type of singing.

Although Ronstadt had not started out to be a pop-rock singer, she had nonetheless made a career of it, something that continued to surprise her. Her true musical roots were planted with the help of her father, who exposed her to a variety of music, including the melodies of Gilbert and Sullivan. She remembered being endlessly entertained by the rolling, tumbling tunefulness of *HMS Pinafore*, a time-honored operetta written by the English team. As she once said, "I never sang rock 'n' roll until I was sixteen or seventeen. So for me it was the biggest left turn I took in my whole musical career, because I started out as a folk-music artist. All the stuff I did, including Gilbert and Sullivan, came from our living room when I was growing up as a child." Her sudden involvement in the Papp production was a dream come true because it also brought back some of the happiest memories of Ronstadt's childhood. It also required her to work harder than ever to strengthen her voice and fine-tune the soprano tones she needed to sing Mabel.

Ronstadt's technique as a popular singer was actually suited quite well to musical theater work. As a solo performer, she was used to commanding a stage and familiar with the dynamics of playing to a live audience. She had also built her career on her ability to interpret music for an audience, to give songs new life and meaning. Ronstadt's proficiency at communicating the messages and essences of the songs she sang was arguably her greatest talent. It was not just her powerful voice, but the way that voice could convey emotion and sentiment that had led to her superstardom. Both Ronstadt and Papp fervently hoped that the leap from a rocker's stance to that of playing a delicate damsel from a bygone century would not be too difficult. As Ronstadt said, "From the very first day everyone knew I had been thrown into the water with no life jacket." And the fear of acting was still palpable for Ronstadt, who said, "I was never even in a high school play. I never did anything before except stand in front of a microphone and sing."

Just how would Ronstadt bridge the gap between her tough-but-tender rock persona and the sweetly innocent character that was Mabel? As she explained it, "Rock and roll is fiercely defensive —you try to do everything with a lot of conviction and defiance. Mabel, on the other hand, has a Victorian personality —she really is an innocent little maiden. That shows in the songs—you simply have to make a different face to make a different sound and that automatically dictates the attitude. You stand more upright and there's a lift to your whole countenance. It gives you a little more ladylike demeanor."

Mabel's purity was also characterized by the key in which her songs were sung. Fully one entire octave above Ronstadt's normal range, the part of Mabel utilized a high coloratura that was extremely demanding for the husky-throated singer. For the first time, Ronstadt decided that singing lessons were an important part of her new musical education. As she told a reporter, "I'm really not trained to sing, but I'm taking lessons now. I have the range for the role, I can reach all the high notes, but I didn't have the technique to project it. Now I have to get on the Nautilus machine for throats."

Marge Rivingston, a New York vocal teacher who coached Ronstadt for her performances, was certain that learning to sing the higher notes forcefully would not be a problem for the singer. As Rivingston pointed out, "While opera singers hardly ever have a chance to experience themselves from the 'outside,' rock singers are tuned to their own voices. They spend hours on end in recording studios hearing playbacks of themselves." But although Ronstadt's lovely soprano was without question improving, she was still self-deprecating when it came to the quality of her own voice. As she said of her learning process for *Pirates*, "My head range isn't really that developed because I haven't used it since I was about sixteen. I have notes that stick up there. It's like someone's pouring ketchup out of a bottle and you start to shake it and it won't come out and then all of a sudden it comes out in a big blat."

Other *Pirates of Penzance* actors included the then-rising star and Tony Award winner Kevin Kline, teen-pop singer Rex Smith, and British actor Patricia Routledge. The pairing of Linda Ronstadt and Rex Smith in the prominent roles of Mabel and Frederic was very deliberate on the part of Joseph Papp. He had a singular vision in mind for this reintroduction of an art form that was quickly being forgotten by generations raised on popular music. Said Papp, "We wanted to bring this classic into a more popular arena, and bring in certain performers who would attract people who would not ordinarily go to Gilbert and Sullivan." It was a unique strategy among show producers and one that has since opened the doors of opportunity for rock personalities who wish to experiment with theater. But for Ronstadt, Papp's vision translated into one very important thing: having some fun. As she says, "I really like to sing. So this is perfect because I'm not the most important character in the cast by far. Patricia Routledge, Kevin Kline, George Rose, and Tony Azito are the most important because they carry the comedy, and they're all brilliant. We've got these traditional pillars of the theater, all revered and respected, and then there's Rex and me, stumbling around."

There were also some significant adjustments for Ronstadt to make while rehearsing for *Pirates*. She was more than familiar with the way things worked in the

Although some scoffed at the notion of a rock 'n' roll singer performing a sophisticated operetta such as Pirates of Penzance, Ronstadt's costar, George Rose, found her more than able and always professional in her approach. In Rose's opinion, Ronstadt had the kind of talent that would enable her to succeed in any musical genre.

world of rock, but, she said, "I don't know all the protocol of this one yet. Like in my business there's regular time and there's rock and roll time—I usually sleep till 5 in the afternoon, go down to the gig, stagger on stage and scream. This is so much less casual—I have singing lessons at ten in the morning, and you're really expected to be on time."

There was also the little matter of learning how to move around a stage according to a plan. Ronstadt had always had trouble being mobile onstage, even when she was feeling terrific, and having to move while singing Mabel was daunting. She complained that it was hard to remember where she was supposed to be at any given time. Often, she found herself standing in the area marked "Orchestra Pit" at the end of a song.

And because she wasn't able to tap out the time of the music on her hips, as she often did during her own shows, she couldn't figure out what to do with her hands.

Also, as Kevin Kline thoughtfully volunteered during one rehearsal, "This is Gilbert and Sullivan, Linda, you can't say 'Git!'" But director Wilford Leach worked overtime to make things easier for the stars who were not used to cleaning up their accents, following instructions for blocking, and acting dramatically.

Ronstadt admitted to having some of her own ideas about the way the character of Mabel should be played. Leach encouraged her to discover a way to get closer to Mabel, to understand her more fully, thereby bringing more of herself to the role. Although Ronstadt's solution was somewhat surprising, it appeared to make all the difference to her. As she said, "I've started listening a lot to the recording of *Snow White and the Seven Dwarfs*. Snow White is a character I've always been fascinated with. I love her voice, it's the most exquisite, tiny soprano. I'll never be an operatic soprano, so I might as well be a tiny soprano. I've patterned Mabel on Snow White because she's really sweet-natured and very forgiving, and genuinely innocent, but not naive. And at the same time that she's proper and victorian, she's also gutsy." Ronstadt realized her choice of role models was peculiar, but with her usual overabundance of humility she said, "It's funny, because I realize I'm talking about a cartoon character, but I'm convinced this is the right one. I've always sort of thought of myself as a cartoon character anyway."

The reviews for *Pirates of Penzance* were uniformly good, and it became the surprise hit of the Public Theater's season. Reviewers praised Ronstadt's delicate performance which, after all, was not so far from her real-life self. After the summer months, *Pirates* moved to Broadway, where it ran for two more years, with Ronstadt in the title role for as long as her commitments would allow. When the show closed, Ronstadt found she had done what she set out to accomplish. As she said, "I did it for fun and I'm glad I did, but I've spent all my life trying to learn to be a singer, and I have no desire to finish my career as an actress. . . . I feel like I've done my homework and I've done my best—and I don't feel that way about myself very often."

During Ronstadt's hiatus from rock with *Pirates of Penzance* in 1980, Asylum Records released a compilation album called *Linda Ronstadt's Greatest Hits, Volume II.* The record included material from previous albums and sold nicely, thanks to the singer's high profile, although not as well as new material. But it had been two years since Ronstadt had released an album of new songs. This was an uncommonly long period of time for the singer who had averaged an album a year for much of the previous decade. In what was recognized as a rather outlandish move on Ronstadt's part, the singer released *Mad Love* right on the heels of her *Greatest Hits* reissue. In one of Ronstadt's few miscalculations, *Mad Love* was an image revamp along the lines of the current punk-rock musical wave. Sporting a blurry action cover with the singer dressed in black, the album attempted to imitate the pared-down, thrash-rock sound of punk music. Ronstadt had never been much of a leather-and-spandex performer, and her audience wasn't ready to be taken down this unfamiliar road. After a critical lambasting, the album fell off the charts and virtually disappeared.

In 1982, Ronstadt hopped back on track with *Get Closer*, an Asylum offering that returned to the more carefully produced Peter Asher sound. The music was more soul-oriented than much of her previous music had been, incorporating such songs as Joe South's "I Knew You When" and Ike and Tina Turner's "I Think It's Gonna Work Out Fine." The album was strong and straightforward, with very little of the "he done her wrong" romantic posturing that characterized past selections. Instead, it sounded as if Ronstadt had adopted a no-nonsense approach to life, no less heartfelt than before but less victimized. All the vocal work Ronstadt had been doing for *Pirates of Penzance* was paying off in a stronger rock sound, and the critics were definitely impressed. Whereas some female singers from the 1970s had slipped into anonymity, Ronstadt had come back with a vengeance yet again, creating a good, solid rock album in the process.

Although the bulk of concerts on Ronstadt's *Get Closer* tour were well attended, they were not the sellout events that had earmarked her rock career in the 1970s. Her younger fans seemed confused by the singer's sudden switch to operetta, though her loyal over-30 followers still turned out in droves. What seemed clear to Ronstadt, who had just turned 35 herself, was that the rock arena limited her mobility. If she were going to pursue her true interests, she would have to abandon that youth-oriented forum for a longer period of time.

Already, Ronstadt had started working on a new album that would be a major departure from her musical offerings of the past. There were rumors, too, that she had a few more projects in the works with Joseph Papp. She was set to collaborate on a musical cycle called *The Seven Deadly Sins*, a Bertolt Brecht–Kurt Weill composition, but because the music rights were not secured, the project was not definite. Other challenging projects had also begun turning up for the singer who had proven to the world that one of her greatest gifts was versatility.

CHAPTER
SEVEN

FROM POP TO PUCCINI

A new look: Ronstadt as she appeared in the Copa Room of the Sands Hotel & Casino in Atlantic City, New Jersey, in July 1984, fronting the 47-piece Nelson Riddle Orchestra and performing sophisticated pop and jazz standards from the 1940s.

Not content to rest on her already remarkable laurels, Ronstadt continued to explore new areas of her talent and follow her dreams. Performing *Pirates of Penzance* had been extremely invigorating for her, opening up, as it did, possibilities for new ventures. One of these grew from a meeting with record producer Jerry Wexler in his Long Island home, on a sunny summer afternoon. Ronstadt and Wexler chatted as they listened to the velvety voice of recording artist Mildred Bailey, a big-band jazz singer from the 1930s. As Ronstadt said of Bailey, who had long been one of her favorites, "She had a particular diction that was very precise and very American, and there was this innocent sexuality that I loved. When I said I wanted to sing like that, Jerry said that the best way was to get a pianist and learn how those songs are done. I decided to tape myself at the same time, to check my progress." What resulted from Ronstadt's interest was a jazzy-sounding album of standard melodies from the 1930s and 1940s. Wexler helped Ronstadt put together a small band for her experiment, but the recordings were never released; still, Ronstadt's urge to create a record with cover versions of classic songs by Cole Porter, Irving Berlin, and others had clearly become an obsession.

When it came to putting this new style of album together, Ronstadt's first consideration was choosing an arranger for the elegant, old-fashioned song material. Longtime friend Randy Newman, who had written so many songs for her in the past, was one of her choices. His career had blossomed, branching out from songwriting into arranging and producing other artists' work. Newman was, however, busy with a previous recording commitment, so Ronstadt decided to approach her only other choice, the legendary Nelson Riddle. Riddle had arranged Frank Sinatra's most poignant songs and had recently finished *The Best Is Yet To Come*, an album by the great jazz singer Ella Fitzgerald. Ronstadt knew that working with Nelson Riddle would be the key to her success in handling the well-known and difficult tunes she had in mind. As she said, "When I first heard Frank Sinatra's *Only the Lonely* album, which [Nelson] had arranged, I was only seventeen and it was the middle of the folk era. We weren't supposed to be listening to stuff like that, but I just played it to death. There's something very different between Nelson's arrange-

Record producer Jerry Wexler became a legend in the music industry through his work with such seminal artists as Ray Charles, Aretha Franklin, and Bob Dylan. It was Wexler who piqued Ronstadt's interest in the torch songs and jazzy ballads that she recorded on her albums What's New, Lush Life, *and* For Sentimental Reasons.

ments and Montovani, for instance. Nelson's not sugary. The funk is still there, somehow."

Riddle agreed to help, and the album that resulted from their cooperation, *What's New*, was a hugely popular record that displayed Ronstadt's talent as a song stylist in all its glory. Ronstadt also credits Wexler with having given her the advice she needed to do justice to the famous songs. As she said, "I really wanted the melodic aspect of that era to come through. One thing Jerry Wexler taught me was that if you've got a sexy or a torchy song, you mustn't attitudinize on top of it, because it sounds redundant. With rock 'n' roll, on the other hand, everything goes, which is one reason why it's so joyously wonderful. Singing rock, you can look someone in the eye and tell them one thing and insinuate the dead opposite, and have the message come through as clear as though you just typed it up and handed it to them. The older music has to be handled with much more control."

What's New, which featured such dreamy ballads as "Someone To Watch Over Me," "What'll I Do," and "Lover Man," a torchy offering that jazz singer Billie Holiday made famous, was an overnight sensation. Again, Ronstadt had broken the unspoken code of rock performers by reaching back into music history to appropriate the style of another age. But this time it worked so well that other artists such as soul singer Chaka Kahn and rocker Rickie Lee Jones, rushed to do their own albums of standards. Radio airwaves were filled with the songs from *What's New* almost immediately after its release, and it was obvious that the album had struck a strong chord among listeners. As Ronstadt mused, "People seem grateful for this album in a way I've never experienced before. Older people finally feel included and validated in some way. I think their feelings were hurt in the sixties when our generation rebelled. . . . I'd be delighted to think that this record, in its own little way, has helped build a bridge back." The album received airplay from classical radio stations, which were attracted to the music and touch of Nelson Riddle, as well as from rock-oriented stations, which were attracted to Ronstadt.

Ronstadt also credits the appeal of *What's New* to the fact that the album grew out of her own intense personal interest in the music. The desire to create the album had been so strong that listeners were undoubtedly able to hear the sincerity of the singer's intentions in her voice. This ability to translate passion into something that can actually be heard has always been Ronstadt's strongest gift; the emotion behind the melodic strains of *What's New* proved no exception to the rule. Ronstadt has explained her philosophy about making the album this way: "The mythographer Joseph Campbell invented a wonderful phrase— 'following your bliss.' He wrote that doing what made you feel blissful was really the only guideline for how to live your life and stay out of trouble.... There was no more blissful musical experience than singing those songs with Nelson's arrangements."

Ronstadt's work with arranger Nelson Riddle, who was best known for his work on Frank Sinatra's "comeback" albums of the 1950s, has been one of the most successful artistic collaborations of her career.

Ronstadt soon took her show on the road, performing the songs from *What's New* with a 47-piece orchestra conducted by Riddle himself. Never before had a singer with such an indelible pedigree as a rock performer appeared on stage to sing music that predated the 1950s. It was an exciting series of shows that featured Ronstadt dressed in period organdy and chiffon gowns, as well as a group of backup singers called the Step Sisters. Liza Edwards, another backup singer who was often featured in Ronstadt's rock shows, sang with Ronstadt and the Step Sisters to create a sound Ronstadt described as "the Andrews Sisters plus two." Ronstadt discovered the Step Sisters after hearing them sing in a Los Angeles restaurant and although their sound was a departure from the mellower Riddle tunes, their numbers together added spice to the shows.

Because Ronstadt had immersed herself so completely in the music of the past, she could not be sure what her next project would be. As she told an interviewer, "I'm not abandoning rock and roll, but there are more things that I want to communicate, more facets to my personality than I can get out in the kinds of songs I've been singing." Stepping away from rock was the only way Ronstadt felt she could really grow up and begin to nurture her growing expertise. Her ability to choose projects that both showcased her talents and gained public acceptance was truly impressive. When asked how she knew there would be renewed interest in these areas, Ronstadt said, "I just know that I hear stuff and I want to do it. It's the same as when I was little and listened to Hank Williams. That was one of the things that inspired me to sing."

As a performer with the determination to explore new artistic territory, Ronstadt has few peers. Composer Philip Glass has applauded Ronstadt for her apparent fearlessness in taking on new challenges.

Having worked with her on two of his own compositions, "Songs from Liquid Days" and "1,000 Airplanes
on the Roof," he is well qualified to pass judgment. As Glass said, "People don't appreciate how
courageous she is. . . . This is a woman who'll try
her talents out. She's a very serious musician. The
great thing about her is that she'll try anything."
His opinion was more than supported by an an-
nouncement in 1984 that Ronstadt had agreed to
star in the New York Shakespeare Festival revival of
Giacomo Puccini's opera *La Bohème*.

Based on the French author Henri Murger's *Scènes
de la vie de Bohème*, *La Bohème* is a romantic tale of
artistic life in Paris during the early 19th century. For
the Joseph Papp production, the libretto was translated
from Puccini's native Italian into English, and the
language was updated to include more modern ex-
pressions. Interestingly enough, the original Murger
version seems to depict the heroine, Mimí, as bearing

*Avant-garde composer
Philip Glass, with whom
Ronstadt worked during
the 1980s, is just one of
many musicians who has
praised her willingness to
test her artistic limits.*

a remarkable physical resemblance to Linda Ronstadt. As Murger describes the character, "Her face reminded one of some sketch of high-born beauty . . . her clear complexion had the white, velvety bloom of the camellia." And Ronstadt's petite delicacy was just right for the consumptive Mimí's heartbreaking fragility.

The offer to play Mimí came once again at the behest of Joseph Papp, Wilford Leach, and the Public Theater, continuing a relationship forged with *Pirates of Penzance*. The working experience between Papp and Ronstadt had been so fruitful the first time around that the team decided to try and repeat their earlier success. Ronstadt shared the part of Mimí, a poverty-stricken seamstress, with two other singers, Patti Cohenour and Caroline Peyton. The role was terribly demanding, requiring a performer to sing steadily in the middle ranges of the soprano voice. It was thought that switching off from night to night would help alleviate some of the vocal stress of singing in such a high and variable key. As Ronstadt described it, "High C is easy for me. I look forward to it every

Ronstadt's performance as Mimí in the New York Public Theater's production of the Puccini opera La Bohème *was not as well received as her work in* Pirates of Penzance, *and she was the first to acknowledge the immense challenges the role presented her.*

night. I can sing real high and I can sing on the bottom. But shifting gears from low to high is the hard thing. No wonder singers call that middle break the Devil's Canyon!"

The Papp production of *La Bohème* was a slightly updated version of the Puccini opera. The music was kept close to that of the original, but with a scaled-back orchestra consisting of only 12 musicians. The time period was also adjusted so that the action would take place in the café society of the 1890s, a jump forward from its previous time setting in the 1830s. And following the strategy of *Pirates of Penzance*, Papp cast Ronstadt opposite another pop-country singer, Gary Morris. A renowned Nashville musician, Morris was also taking a big chance playing the role of Rodolfo, a pivotal character in the opera. His twangy Tennessee accent was a drawback, though his reportedly "teddybearish" presence did much to offset any ill effects of the southern inflection. Morris also split his time with actor-singer David Carroll, making for an extremely mobile lineup as well as a relatively inexperienced one. Almost all the players in *La Bohème* had never been in an opera before; in fact, a few had never even heard one. A musician was reported to have said during the early days of rehearsal, "Isn't there any dialogue in this show?"

Ronstadt's anxious feelings about singing in an operatic style prompted her to take dramatic steps to strengthen her vocal range. For instance, she increased the frequency of the voice lessons, which had now become part of her standard operating procedure. But there were other problems that needed to be addressed. Because she could not read music, Ronstadt tape-recorded rehearsals in order to "parrot," as she put it, the phrasing of the other singers. Composer Allen Shawn also extended a helping hand by walking Ronstadt through the music, step by step. She characterized Shawn as one of her "real guiding heroes" for his attention to making sure she understood the requirements for singing Mimí.

But all Ronstadt could hope for was that she would be able to learn enough to sing Mimí capably. As she said, "I've always known my voice could make more kinds of sounds than it did. If I'd been born at the beginning of the nineteenth century, I'd definitely have been an opera singer; but when I was a teen-ager, I loved Little Richard so much all I ever wanted to do was sound like him." At this stage of the game, there was a limited amount she could do to improve the physical strength of her voice in the period of time she had. Singing with Nelson Riddle's orchestra had made her voice sturdier and more pliant, but she simply did not have the training to force power into her high notes.

It was an uphill struggle, though, and ultimately *La Bohème* was not received with the same tumultuous praise *Pirates* had garnered. Frank Rich, an influential theater critic for the *New York Times*, admired Ronstadt's bravery in attacking the role but thought she had forced "her lovely soprano into places where nature or training had not yet permitted it to go." He also complimented Ronstadt's ability to give audiences "the fragrance if not the beauty of the gorgeous melodies." Rich cited the production as a whole as not quite successful in achieving its aim to update opera for a new set of listeners, and *La Bohème* did not enjoy a very long run.

Meanwhile, Ronstadt had once again returned to the studio with Nelson Riddle to create a second album tailored along the same lines as *What's New*. Called *Lush Life* and featuring a campy, 1940s-style album cover showing Ronstadt walking two enormous dogs and toting a large hatbox, the new offering picked up where the previous one left off. Riddle's arrangements again brought out the best in Ronstadt's voice, showcasing the gentle and compelling melodies she had chosen to cover. The mood on her newest album was also less lovelorn than *What's New*, sounding decidedly more upbeat and bold. Ronstadt, too, sounded more comfortable and willing to stretch even more than she had on the previous album.

It was now 1986, and Ronstadt was settling down after a series of dramatic changes in her personal life. After beginning her work on *Pirates of Penzance*, Ronstadt had bought a three-bedroom apartment on Manhattan's Upper West Side. She had become enamored with the energy and variety that New York offered and knew that it was the best place for her to pursue her theater interests. The city was also a wonderfully anonymous environment for Ronstadt, who disliked being recognized as a celebrity. Manhattan's rough exterior also posed a more universal problem for Ronstadt, who once said humorously, "New York doesn't care about stars. It's just being female in the street. If you had your hair in rollers, mayonnaise smeared all over your face and a rhinoceros on a leash, you'd still get hit on!"

But after only a few years, she realized that New York would never really feel like home. Following the call of family and familiarity, Ronstadt returned to California and bought a house outside San Francisco. Using that as her home base, she was free to travel easily to Arizona and to spend quality time in New York. Having a safe haven had always been of the utmost importance to Ronstadt, as was being close to her parents, brothers, and sister, whose love provided the sustenance she needed.

Also, toward the end of 1986 Ronstadt released two albums, both of great significance to audiences and to herself. The first one to arrive was the third in the Nelson Riddle series, called *For Sentimental*

Reasons. A boxed set of all three albums was released in conjunction with the record, the last one she would make with Riddle, who had been suffering from a liver ailment for a long time and died in 1985 at age 64, shortly before the recording sessions of *For Sentimental Reasons* were completed. The boxed set was called *'Round Midnight: The Nelson Riddle Sessions* and was a tremendous seller, combining the best of Ronstadt's work with the famous arranger. *For Sentimental Reasons* had also become a big hit on its own, mainly for the more visible role Ronstadt took in guiding the direction of the record.

Where Ronstadt had previously relied on lushly orchestral song introductions, *For Sentimental Reasons* saw the singer leading the way into the melodies with her voice. Clearly, she was becoming more comfortable with her own talents as a song stylist. The album contained two bouncy, up-tempo tunes, "Straighten Up and Fly Right," a standard made popular by Nat King Cole, and "Am I Blue," sung as a jazzy duet with James Taylor. Strangely, the only song Nelson Riddle admitted to not being satisfied with in regard to his own arrangements was the album's title song. "(I Love You) for Sentimental Reasons" was notoriously tricky, and Riddle had decided to include some 1950s doo-wop vocal backgrounds that did not work as well as his simpler arrangements.

The boxed set *'Round Midnight* seemed to represent a kind of closure to the project Ronstadt had worked on so steadfastly. With Riddle's death she had lost a vital partner in realizing the musical vision she wanted to achieve. When asked if there was a possibility for another album of standards in the future, Ronstadt replied, "I don't think I could do it anymore without Nelson. He was irreplaceable. Nobody put jazz in the pop orchestra the way he did. . . . While we were working on the album, I could tell by his coloring that Nelson was very ill, though I had no idea he only had a few weeks left." They had actually planned a more elaborate project with *For Sentimental Reasons*. It was intended as a double-album-set, with the second disk being a collection of fine old Afro-Cuban and bossa nova–style songs. Brazilian composer and band-leader Antonio Carlos Jobim was to have collaborated on the compilation, and it surely would have been one of the more exciting musical offerings of the year. But Riddle died almost before they could com-

The album Trio, *recorded with her fellow queens of country music Dolly Parton (center) and Emmylou Harris (right), represented Ronstadt's return to the deeply rooted American music with which she had grown up.*

plete the first album; in fact, Ronstadt said, "we had to scramble to do what we did."

After the tepid reviews Ronstadt had garnered for her performance as Mimí, the tumultuous acclaim and incredible airplay *What's New*, *Lush Life*, and *For Sentimental Reasons* received was welcome indeed. Ronstadt had been working without a break since the early 1980s and still had so many obligations to fulfill that it seemed as if she would never be able to rest. But rest was not her goal just yet, because her next project had been a true labor of love. After many years of thwarted beginnings and unfinished sessions, her second album of 1986 was being released. Called *Trio*, it was the album she had always wanted to make and the one she has since called her favorite.

Along with her good friends Emmylou Harris and Dolly Parton, Ronstadt recorded *Trio* as a delightful collection of old folk tunes that the three most famous women in country music sang together. *Trio*'s bumpy beginnings back in 1978 were not caused by any indecision on the part of the singers. Parton, Harris, and Ronstadt were tremendously excited by the idea and ready to leap in and start recording immediately. The main difficulty lay in the fact that each woman was at the peak of her career, and the timing for a joint project was not right. After the first attempt to bring it all together, the trio recorded a few songs, but previous commitments forced them to call a halt. Happily, their second try in 1986 was successful.

The voices of Parton, Ronstadt, and Harris blended in a remarkably successful manner. By highlighting each other's strong points and making up for any weaknesses, the three singers managed to fill in all the missing pieces. After almost eight years of discussion and planning, *Trio* effectively encompassed the ideas of each of the artists. Although the three actually sing in unison as equal partners for only two of the songs, the rest of the melodies are adapted as leader-support harmony arrangements. Ronstadt has a fine solo turn with the song "Telling Me Lies," written by old friend Linda Thompson and backed up with beautiful vocals by Parton and Harris. Dolly Parton sings Johnny Russell's "Making Plans," and Emmylou Harris has a fine moment with "My Dear Companion," a tune written by Jean Ritchie. Throughout, background vocals are contributed by the two singers who do not carry the lead, and the effect is haunting.

Also, because of the star-power of Parton, Harris, and Ronstadt, the assemblage of session musicians was the finest to be had anywhere. Guitarists Albert Lee and Ry Cooder, who often played in Ronstadt's back-up band, appeared on the album, as did Nashville regular Mark O'Connor and bluegrass specialist John Starling. Ironically, legal entanglements were the only obstacles that threatened to waylay the album's progress. The complications arising from negotiations between three different managers and record companies were almost laughable. Because all the artists cared about was getting the album done, they were spared the constant legal tussles and negotiations occurring behind the scenes. Each woman also brought her own set of emotional difficulties; Parton and Ronstadt had both suffered from slight health problems in the previous year, and Harris was in the midst of a painful child-custody battle. Dolly Parton summed it all up by joking to a reporter in her characteristic Tennessee accent, "You know how hard it is to get three women together and get their schedules to work?!"

Once underway, the sessions were comfortable and creative. Parton, Ronstadt, and Harris had all known each other for such a long time that for them it was like working with their own sisters. Ronstadt had first met Harris while she was touring with Neil

Young so many years before in the early 1970s. Back then, as Dolly Parton recalled, "Linda was just beginning to become popular. . . . Then I came to Los Angeles and she and Emmy were friends already. When they met, I guess they'd discussed me. So when I got to L.A., Emmy invited me to her house and she invited Linda, too. It was the first time we'd ever sung together, and it sounded so good and so natural that we wanted to record it." Although it took them years to do, their effort was worth the wait. *Trio* went on to win the Grammy Award that year for Best Country Performance by a Duo or Group.

For Ronstadt, the return to the sweeter and gentler sound of country music was a relief after the vocal acrobatics she had been tackling since 1980. The style had always been one of her favorites and the success of such country acts as the Judds and Reba McEntire was making the music commercially viable again. But far beyond album sales, *Trio* was a pet project for all three singers and one they were all individually proud of. Even though Parton and Ronstadt made the album at a time when their musical styles could not have been further from country, it was a triumphant return to the genre that gave them their start. As Parton said, "It's the most natural thing in the world! Somebody said, 'Oh, it must be nice getting back to your roots.' But I never left 'em!"

The Songs of Her Father

Musical influences are often discussed in terms of style, as if a particular kind of music could explain the progression of an artist's career. Most of the time, however, it is not as much the kind of music as it is the messenger that provides the influence. Such performers such as Elvis Presley and Jerry Lee Lewis held sway over a generation of young musicians entranced as much by their personalities as by their songs. It seems natural, then, that the single greatest influence on Linda Ronstadt's music was her father, Gilbert, a man who made sure from the very beginning that music was a part of his children's lives. Through the years, Linda Ronstadt sampled many kinds of melodic styles, running the gamut from country and rock to the big-band sound and opera, then back again. The only area she had not yet explored as an artist was, oddly enough, the one that may have been closest to her heart: the grand, sweeping and intensely poignant style of Mexican mariachi music—the songs of her father's boyhood.

Mariachi music originated in the northwestern states of Mexico, particularly Jalisco. It began as a folk tradition that gradually became more complex as it grew in popularity, becoming almost orchestral in sound by the 1920s and 1930s. The style became even more popular when Mexican cowboy movies appropriated the music and made it available to larger audiences. According to a theory by the journalist Pete Hamill, the word *mariachi* itself might be a corruption of the French word *mariage*, or "marriage." French troops were posted in Mexico during the years 1861-67, and small Mexican bands were often hired to play at weddings and other occasions. From these early days the basic style has remained the same—formal yet full of joy and expressiveness. Most recently, mariachi bands have been comprised of *vihuelas* (five-string guitars), one or two *guitarrones* (six-string bass guitars), one or more trumpets, and a violin. Other instruments are sometimes included, but strings typically dominate the sound. Mariachi music was also often paired with dance, and for this reason it is an extremely ceremonious style that underscores the theatricality of the lyrics.

The music also provided another influential figure in the development of Linda Ronstadt's singing style—Lola Beltran, arguably Mexico's best-loved singer of all time. Beltran became famous for her commanding vocal style in the 1920s and 1930s, and Ronstadt has often cited the singer as being her greatest inspiration. As Ronstadt once commented, "I've always tried to sing like her, but you can hear it most clearly on my earliest records like 'Different Drum' in which I made a conscious effort to recreate her vocal tone. Later, in my version of 'Blue Bayou,' I used the falsetto at the end which is a Mexican vocal trick. Unfortunately, the English language can only accommodate these sounds to a limited extent."

Beltran's music continued to be of tremendous personal importance to Ronstadt even as her career guided her in different directions. Still, it seemed only a matter of time before Ronstadt would have to pursue the music that was in her heart. All of her previous efforts, even her songs with Nelson Riddle, had been calculated to a certain extent. Ronstadt has pointed out that her need to attain ever greater technical proficiency might have come from the Dutch side of her, from her mother. Ronstadt's next album, *Canciones de Mi Padre* (Songs of My Father), was an entirely different matter because, as she has said, "these songs are a complete release of that other part of my heart. It's just my Dad."

Canciones de Mi Padre came together in an interesting way for Ronstadt, who was introduced to the mariachi musicians she had always longed to perform with in her hometown of Tucson. Ronstadt and her father had decided to take part in a mariachi festival being held there and were delighted to find that the oldest continuing mariachi group, Mariachi Vargas de Tecalitlán, had also been invited. As Ronstadt remembered, "The Mariachi Vargas is the best in the world, but I could never figure out how to approach them. They don't know me or rock and roll from Adam, and for a woman to go down to Mexico—a male society—is not considered proper. Even now when I go I take my father or brother!"

The Tucson festival also introduced Ronstadt to Rubén Fuentes, perhaps the only man who could successfully coach her to sing the songs properly. Even though she had grown up knowing much of the music, the training her voice required to take on the intricate melody structures was demanding. And there was again the matter of phrasing, something she had worked on rigorously with Nelson Riddle. As Ronstadt described it, "I have a lot of northernisms. They are speech mannerisms that people who have lived across the Mexican border for a couple of generations have adopted. It was hard work unlearning them, and Rubén was a merciless teacher."

The struggle was well worth the result. Not only was *Canciones de Mi Padre* declared Linda Ronstadt's finest album, but it also sold amazingly well for a foreign language offering. In the first weeks of its release, the album hit number 55 on the *Billboard* charts and went gold, Ronstadt's 15th record to do so, with sales of more than 500,000 copies—not bad for a musical offering with lyrics most North Americans could not understand. The album also won Ronstadt another Grammy for Best Performance by a Mexican American, a brand-new category for the awards ceremony.

Ronstadt soon crafted a show around the songs from *Canciones de Mi Padre* with help from talented set designer Tony Walton, lighting expert Jules Fisher, and ex–San Francisco Ballet choreographer Michael Smuin. Ronstadt has credited Smuin with sharing her initial vision about doing the show. As she said, Smuin "was one of the few people who didn't give me that RCA dog look," as if he did not understand what she had in mind. The wonderful comic-strip sets were a huge success, as was the lighting, which brought out the best in both the pastel desert hues of the background and the boldy colored costumes of the cast members. All in all, the show was a marvelous distillation of all the joyous and vibrant elements that characterize Mexico.

The unprecedented success of *Canciones de Mi Padre,* both as an album and as a sublime piece of musical theater, brought Ronstadt new attention. She was fast becoming known as one of the only women artists in history to celebrate the splendor of regional music. This interest led to another of her most distinctive albums.

Back in the mid-1980s, Ronstadt traveled to New Orleans to see the Neville Brothers, a soulful, blues-inflected band considered one of the local treasures of Louisiana. The Neville Brothers had long been among Ronstadt's favorite musicians. Aaron Neville's falsetto had already become legendary in the music industry, and Ronstadt was excited about seeing the band perform live. She had no idea Aaron Neville was planning a surprise for her during the show. As she recalled, "I was flabbergasted when he dedicated a song to me and invited me up on stage to sing a doo-wop medley. I thought our voices sounded really good together and so did he." A few months later, Neville called Ronstadt and asked if she would appear with him at a New Orleans benefit for the homeless. Ronstadt happily accepted, and the two performed "Ave Maria" together, which was the only song both of them knew. After that show, Ronstadt said, "I just blurted out that I wanted to make a record with him, and he said sure."

Several years later, in 1989, their chance collaboration paid off in the form of an album called *Cry Like a Rainstorm, Howl Like the Wind*. The album was a departure from the eclectic musical styles of Ronstadt's past few records, focusing once again on pop-rock sounds for the first time in seven years. But there was still the problem of finding material that was suitable for both Ronstadt's and Aaron Neville's voices and singing styles. As Ronstadt commented, "If there's anything I don't sing, it's New Orleans rhythm-and-blues, and he's as firmly in that bag as you can get. My feeling was that with the right songs we could swim from opposite shores and meet on an island in the middle."

The solution was to choose no more than four songs for Ronstadt and Neville to perform as duets. This resulted in the first single released from the album, "Don't Know Much," which garnered Ronstadt and Neville a Grammy for Best Pop Performance by a Duo or Group. The other three songs, "All

In 1990, Ronstadt received a Grammy Award for her duet performance of "Don't Know Much" with the New Orleans singer Aaron Neville. Future albums are certain to garner her even more accolades.

My Life," "When Something Is Wrong with My Baby," and "I Need You," were all well received. Former Beach Boy Brian Wilson also appeared on *Cry Like a Rainstorm*, providing the backup vocals for the cut that Ronstadt calls her favorite from the album. The song, "Adios," a mournful ballad written by Jimmy Webb, is the melody Ronstadt calls her own kind of good-bye to Los Angeles. She had come to the decision that although her life in that city had been rich, she could never live there again. *Cry Like a Rainstorm* surprised everyone involved by going platinum soon after its release, selling 2 million copies in a matter of weeks.

The 1991 Christmas season was a period of high visibility and good press for Ronstadt. First, she finally released her promised follow-up album to *Canciones de Mi Padre*, called *Más Canciones* (More Songs). Ronstadt was asked why she released a second volume of mariachi music so shortly after the big success of her pop album. Her simple answer was, "The reason I did it was selfish. I had started to make a record in English, but I didn't like it and put it away. I found myself sleeping and dreaming in Spanish, and these songs were driving me crazy. I kept waking up in the middle of the night thinking that the musicians who know this music are old, and if they go I won't have anybody to help me do it. I didn't dare put it off another minute." The real difference between *Más Canciones* and its predecessor is that it is a family affair. Ronstadt is joined on many of the vocal trios by her brothers, Pete and Mike, and for this album, the arrangements are kept as simple as the ones the family sang in their Tucson living room. Ronstadt also felt she had to do the album, in part, as a result of the kind of regional touring she had been doing for the previous two years.

Because of the elaborate nature of the sets and costumes, the first Canciones de Mi Padre show had played only selected cities. It was also a tremendously expensive show to do, and the price of tickets unfortunately reflected those costs. But Ronstadt was disappointed to realize that for the most part the very people whose music she was performing could not afford to come and see the songs played live. In an effort to reach a wider audience, she began exploring the possibilities of doing a less extravagant version of the show in the Southwest. As she said, "I went in pursuit of the $10 ticket and found the only way to do it was with no sound, no lights, two musicians, two dancers, and a horse. For the last two years I've been doing it all over the place: at dance halls down by the border and at state fairs, rodeos, and at Mexican horse shows called charreadas. . . . Three generations of Mexican-Americans would show up. It was an exhilarating experience to see a 75-year-old grandmother start to sing a song from the twenties and thirties, and I would sense that this was a song she had courted to."

Perhaps even more visible than her touring and the *Más Canciones* release was Ronstadt's holiday-season acting appearance as a part of Public Tele-

vision's "Great Performances" series. Cast as the Arch-
angel San Miguel, defender of the innocent and faith-
ful, Ronstadt was one of the stars of *La Pastorela* (The
Shepherd's Tale), a Mexican folktale based on the story
of the birth of Jesus Christ. Luis Valdez, director of the
films *La Bamba* and *Zoot Suit*, was a filmmaker
Ronstadt had admired for some time. The chance to
work with him on such a fun and uplifting project was
impossible to turn down, even though her schedule
was more hectic than ever. Ronstadt's time was so
tight that she was forced to ask Valdez, "Can you do
my scenes in two days?" He said he could.

The Mexican-style Christmas fantasy, which
deftly mixed Spanish and English elements, followed
the progress of a ragtag band of shepherds on their
way to Bethlehem. Valdez included ideas from *The
Wizard of Oz* in *La Pastorela*, framing the plot with the
story of a young Mexican girl whose bump on the
head during a Christmas pageant gets the merry action underway. Ronstadt makes her first appearance to
this young girl, who finds herself transformed into
one of a group of shepherds traveling to the Holy
Land to pay homage to the baby Jesus. Demons sent
by Lucifer, played by Robert Beltran, try to impede
the shepherds' progress, with comic results. Come-
dians Paul Rodriguez and Cheech Marin play two of
the more obnoxious of these demons, who often
make their appearance riding motorcycles. Ronstadt,
as the determined angel San Miguel, repeatedly res-
cues the shepherds from the evil demons, flying down
from the heavens dressed in golden armor and wield-
ing a righteous sword and a powerful song.

With *La Pastorela*, Ronstadt showed style and
grace before the cameras, but she continued to claim
she had no interest in pursuing any kind of acting
career. As she has said, "I'm not an actress. I have no
desire to make movies, nor am I interested in doing a

video. I like live theater and love musical theater." But clearly she was not ruling out a change of heart. Her sense of identification with Mexico had never been stronger, and she earnestly supported the work of Hispanic artists.

Of course, musical projects were always in Ronstadt's thoughts, and in 1992–93 she developed two new albums. One, a bilingual album of Latin jazz songs, *Frenesí*, covers that style of music from the turn of the century to its heyday in the 1950s. The other record explores a style she called Texas Border music, an amalgam of Mexican and American country-cowboy sounds. The famed accordionist Flaco Jiminez, who appears on *Más Canciones*, was involved in the second album project.

Ronstadt believed that the reception of these albums would be as positive as that of her mariachi records. After all, she said, "I've been tooting this horn for a long time. American popular music is based on cultural diversity." But she insisted her interest in investigating new genres would not prevent her from making a new pop album again in the future. Whatever Linda Ronstadt's future musical or theatrical venture may be, it will surely reflect the same high standards she has maintained for more than three decades, and undoubtedly will surprise and gratify, because her devoted audience has come to expect the unexpected from her.

SELECTED DISCOGRAPHY

1969	*Hand Sown . . . Home Grown*
1970	*Silk Purse*
1972	*Linda Ronstadt*
1973	*Don't Cry Now*
1974	*Heart Like a Wheel*
	Different Drum
1975	*Prisoner in Disguise*
1976	*Hasten down the Wind*
	Linda Ronstadt's Greatest Hits
1977	*Simple Dreams*
	Blue Bayou
	Retrospective
1978	*Living in the U.S.A.*
1980	*Linda Ronstadt's Greatest Hits, Volume II*
1982	*Get Closer*
1983	*What's New*
1984	*Lush Life*
1986	*For Sentimental Reasons*
	Prime of Life
	Rockfile
1987	*Canciones de Mi Padre*
1989	*Cry Like a Rainstorm, Howl Like the Wind*
1991	*Más Canciones*
1992	*Frenesí*
1993	*Winter Light*
1995	*Feels Like Home*
1996	*Dedicated to the One I Love*
1998	*We Ran*
	Trio II
1999	*Western Wall: The Tucson Sessions*

106

CHRONOLOGY

1946	Born Linda Marie Ronstadt in Tucson, Arizona, on July 15
1960	Meets Bob Kimmel, a Tucson folk musician, while she is still in high school
1964	Arrives in Los Angeles with $30 in her pocket; the Stone Poneys, featuring Ronstadt as lead singer, are signed to Capitol Records
1965	The Stone Poneys' first single, "Some of Shelley's Blues," is released
1967	Capitol Records releases the Stone Poneys' first album, *Evergreen*; the Stone Poneys have their first hit single, "Different Drum"
1968	The Stone Poneys disband and Ronstadt begins her career as a solo artist
1969	Ronstadt releases *Hand Sown . . . Home Grown*, her first solo album
1973	Switches record labels, moving from Capitol Records to Asylum for her fourth album, *Don't Cry Now*; Peter Asher becomes her manager and producer
1974	*Heart Like a Wheel* becomes Ronstadt's first platinum album; Ronstadt wins her first Grammy Award for Best Female Country Vocal Performance
1975	Releases her seventh album, *Prisoner of Disguise*, which quickly becomes a gold record
1976	Releases *Hasten down the Wind*; wins Grammy for Best Pop Female Vocalist; voted Top Female Singer by *Playboy* magazine in both the Pop and Country categories
1977	Releases *Simple Dreams*, another platinum seller that features her first attempt at a harder rock song, the Rolling Stones' "Tumbling Dice"

1980   Joseph Papp casts Linda Ronstadt as Mabel in the Gilbert and Sullivan operetta *Pirates of Penzance*

1983   Ronstadt releases *What's New*, an album of standard 1940s melodies, arranged by veteran bandleader Nelson Riddle

1984   Accepts the role of Mimí in the new Joseph Papp–Wilford Leach production of *La Bohème*

1987   Releases *Canciones de Mi Padre*, an album of Mexican music; wins a Grammy for Best Performance by a Mexican American

1989   Releases *Cry Like a Rainstorm, Howl Like the Wind*; Ronstadt and Aaron Neville win a Grammy for Best Pop performance by a Duo or Group

1991   Ronstadt releases a second volume of Mexican music, *Más Canciones;* appears in the film *La Pastorela*

1993   Wins Grammy Awards for *Más Canciones* and *Frenesí*

1995   Releases *Feels Like Home*

1996   Releases *Dedicated to the One I Love*

1998   Releases *We Ran* and *Trio II* with Dolly Parton and Emmylou Harris

1999   *Trio II* wins a Grammy award; releases *Western Wall: The Tucson Sessions* with Emmylou Harris

FURTHER READING

Bane, Michael. *Who's Who in Rock: Over 1,200 Personalities That Made Rock Happen.* New York: Facts on File, 1981.

Christgau, Robert. *Christgau's Record Guide.* New York: Ticknor & Fields, 1981.

Moore, Mary Ellen. *The Linda Ronstadt Scrapbook.* New York: Grosset & Dunlap, 1978.

Riding, Alan. *Distant Neighbors: A Portrait of the Mexicans.* New York: Vintage, 1986.

Stambler, Irwin. *The Encyclopedia of Pop, Rock, and Soul.* New York: St. Martin's, 1976.

Tudor, Dean, and Nancy Tudor. *Contemporary Popular Music.* New York: Libraries Unlimited, 1979.

———. *The Illustrated Encyclopedia of Country Music.* New York: Harmony, 1977.

INDEX

Asher, Peter, 40, 43, 44, 45, 46–50, 51, 52, 61, 65, 78

Asylum Records, 40, 50, 63, 67, 78

Baez, Joan, 24

Beltran, Lola, 24, 98

Blue Bayou, 67

Boylan, John, 39, 40, 41, 45

Brown, Jerry, 68–70

Canciones de Mi Padre
    performance, 15–19, 99, 103
    recording, 99, 100, 102

Capitol Records, 35, 36, 37, 40, 50, 60, 67

Cohen, Herb, 34, 35, 38, 39, 41

Cry Like a Rainstorm, Howl Like the Wind, 101, 102

Don't Cry Now, 40, 43, 44, 58

Edwards, Kenny, 32, 33, 35, 36, 60, 61

Espinel, Luisa (aunt), 16, 17, 22

Evergreen, 35

Evergreen, Volume II, 35

FM, 67, 68, 71

For Sentimental Reasons, 90, 91, 92, 93

Get Closer, 78, 79

Gilbert and Sullivan, 71, 72, 73, 75, 77

Gold, Andrew, 51, 52, 60, 64, 65

Hand Sown . . . Home Grown, 38

Harris, Emmylou, 50, 57, 58, 59, 93, 94, 95

Hasten down the Wind, 61, 63

Heart Like a Wheel, 50, 51, 52, 55, 60, 67

Kimmel, Bob, 28, 29, 31, 33, 34, 35

La Bohème, 86, 88, 89

La Pastorela, 104

Linda Ronstadt, 39, 67

Linda Ronstadt's Greatest Hits, 63

Linda Ronstadt's Greatest Hits, Volume II, 78

Linda Ronstadt: Stone Poneys and Friends, 36

Living in the U.S.A., 67

Lush Life, 89, 93

Mad Love, 78

Mariachi music, 16, 19, 21, 97, 98, 99, 102, 105

Mariachi Vargas de Tecalitlán, 17, 99

Más Canciones, 102, 103, 105

Mexican music, 15–19, 26, 33, 61, 97

New Union Ramblers, 25, 26

Papp, Joseph, 71, 72, 73, 79, 86, 87, 88

Parton, Dolly, 50, 53, 59, 63, 93, 94, 95

Pirates of Penzance (Gilbert and Sullivan), 71, 72, 75, 78, 79, 81, 87, 88, 90

Presley, Elvis, 24, 67, 68, 97

Prisoner in Disguise, 60, 61

Public Theater, 71, 77, 87

Rancheras, 17, 21

Retrospective, 67

Riddle, Nelson, 82, 83, 84, 85, 89, 90, 91, 92, 99

Ronstadt, Gilbert (father), 21, 22, 23, 24, 61, 97

Ronstadt, Linda
    awards, 52, 61, 62, 95, 100, 101
    and Jerry Brown, 68–70
    childhood, 22–29
    early career, 31–37
    films, 67, 68, 71

opera, 86, 87, 88, 89

recordings, 35, 36, 38, 39, 40, 43, 44, 50, 51, 52, 55, 58–67, 78, 83, 84, 85, 89–95, 99, 100, 101, 102, 103

television, 103–5

theater, 15–19, 71–78, 100

Ronstadt, Mike (brother), 23, 25, 28, 103

Ronstadt, Pete (brother), 23, 24, 25, 28, 103

Ronstadt, Ruthmary Copeman (mother), 22, 23, 70, 99

Ronstadt, Suzi (sister), 23, 24, 25, 28

'Round Midnight: The Nelson Riddle Sessions, 91

Simple Dreams, 63, 65

Souther, John David, 40, 41, 60, 63

Stone Poneys, 33, 34, 35, 36, 60

Trio, 93, 95

Tucson, Arizona, 21, 23, 25, 26, 28, 32, 99, 103

What's New, 83, 84, 85, 89, 90, 93

Young, Neil, 31, 44, 45, 60, 94, 95

MELISSA AMDUR is a New York–based writer with interests ranging from economics to art history. She has worked as an editor in book and magazine publishing, has traveled widely, and is also the author of *Anthony Quinn* in the Chelsea House series HISPANICS OF ACHIEVEMENT.

RODOLFO CARDONA is professor of Spanish and comparative literature at Boston University. A renowned scholar, he has written many works of criticism, including *Ramón, a Study of Gómez de la Serna and His Works* and *Visión del esperpento: Teoría y práctica del esperpento en Valle-Inclán*. Born in San José, Costa Rica, he earned his B.A. and M.A. from Louisiana State University and received a Ph.D. from the University of Washington. He has taught at Case Western Reserve University, the University of Pittsburgh, the University of Texas at Austin, the University of New Mexico, and Harvard University.

JAMES COCKCROFT is currently a visiting professor of Latin American and Caribbean studies at the State University of New York at Albany. A three-time Fulbright scholar, he earned a Ph.D. from Stanford University and has taught at the University of Massachusetts, the University of Vermont, and the University of Connecticut. He is the author or coauthor of numerous books on Latin American subjects, including *Neighbors in Turmoil: Latin America, The Hispanic Experience in the United States: Contemporary Issues and Perspectives*, and *Outlaws in the Promised Land: Mexican Immigrant Workers and America's Future*.

PICTURE CREDITS

AP/Wide World Photos: pp. 18, 40, 51, 68, 71; Courtesy Arizona Historical Society, Tucson: pp. 16, 20, 22, 23; Copyright 1990 Michel Bourguard/LGI: p. 102; Frank Driggs Collection: pp. 25, 42; Copyright 1984 Betty Burke Galella/Ron Galella, Ltd.: pp. 14, 80, 84; Copyright 1978 Ron Galella/Ron Galella, Ltd.: pp. 49, 64, 69; Copyright 1988 Lynn Goldsmith/LGI: p. 86; The Music Division, The New York Public Library, Astor, Lenox, and Tilden Foundations: pp. 27, 58, 82; Michael Ochs Archives, Venice, California: p. 30; Photofest: pp. 32, 38, 54, 56, 59, 96; Jacki Sallow/LGI copyright 1987: p. 92; Copyright 1984 Martha Swope/Martha Swope Photography, Inc.: p. 66; Copyright 1992 Martha Swope/Martha Swope Photography, Inc.: p. 87; Martha Swope Photography, Inc.: p. 76.